To:
Captain James Flanagan
N.Y.P.D.

Jim

With
Great
Memories

George E. Greabeck

Death Penalty: To Be Or Not To Be

GEORGE E GREADER

Preface

Morality in a simplistic form is the difference between right or wrong or good and bad. In a more complex form, morality addresses responsibility embraced with social and legal obligations. Applied to the death penalty, morality is the sociological and justifiable state execution conscientiousness necessary for a psychological imprint of an undaunted society relative to human life for the 'good of the people'.

Recent history has recorded an increase in the death penalty debate as to the best form of punishment for offenders who commit capital crimes. Some argue it is morally wrong to kill someone as punishment for killing another, others strongly believe that it is the best way of deterrence as death makes a lasting impression on future offenders. As such, society and religious sects have become divided on the issue of capital punishments, with some insisting that it has done more good than harm in the maintenance of law and order.

Still others question if the capital punishment is truly a fair branch in justice, why then is it that the offences carrying the death penalty differ from one country to another. Murder cases in the United States attract the death penalty while a lesser crime of sabotaging social amenities like electricity in China attracts the same penalty.

Societal questions demand an explanation for people unfortunate enough to have been executed and later revealed that the crime was committed by a different person(s). What about when a life that we highly claim to cherish and preserve is taken in retribution of an offence committed. Can we say that the justice system is fair enough in its discharge? Can we say the offences tagged as 'death warranted' as their penalties are really worth taking a life; least we forget that some of sentences are based on the judge's belief or frame of mind at the time of pronouncing the judgement on the 'accused.'

Controversies surround the death penalty as a form of punishment for offences tagged 'capital' or 'death warranted'. Presented are thoughts at unravelling numerous conflicting opinions by extensively discussing the terms of the death penalty topic. Various supporting views are presented on the death penalty and its counteracting opinions; on the effects of the death penalty on crime rates in countries; on the various forms of carrying out the execution with emphasis on the use of Lethal Injection in the United States. Questions are asked as to the merits of some cases attracting the death penalty, and the conclusion on how the death penalty was portrayed in those cases.

TABLE OF CONTENTS

INTRODUCTION

Some convicted individuals believe they are innocent and don't belong in prison. The same goes for inmates on death row. Americans have their own opinion. The Gallup polls of 2015 show 64% of Americans favor the death penalty whereas 42% favor Life Without Parole. These figures suggest an argument for change since eight states have abandoned their death sentences as of 2007.

In the United States, executions have fallen to a 25-year low, with 20 executions carried out in 2016 as compared to 98 in 1999. Nevertheless, the number of people on death row in the United States has only slightly declined in the last twenty years, from 3,219 in 1996 to 2,905 in 2016.

Executing an inmate on death row in the US costs considerably more than sending an inmate to prison for life without the possibility for parole. The reason for this is that the inmates on death row are guaranteed a long and very thorough judicial process by the Constitution. Some believe this is done so that the chances of executing an innocent inmate are minimized. Further, studies of the California death penalty system disclose that a death sentence costs at least 18 times as much as a sentence of life without parole.

Allowance for change is a cornerstone of the American government that has lasted over 2 centuries. Americans view change as possible, and that challenges our daily democratic survival. In viewing change, we must ask, do we still need the death penalty? Does the public still want the death penalty or is the death penalty doomed to die itself?

THE RANDY BRAZEAL – RICHARD STOKLEY CASE

Elfrida, Arizona is eighty (80) miles southeast of Tucson, Arizona. On July 7th 1991, during the Elfrida July 4th town celebration, Mandy Meyers and her friend Mary Snyder, both thirteen years old, were camping on an open lot in town with other children while attending a community celebration. During the night, Mandy and Mary were abducted, taken to a remote area where they were raped, beaten, stabbed and killed. Their bodies were thrown into a partly flooded mine shaft. Richard Stokley, aged 38, and Randy Brazeal, aged 19, were also at the campgrounds that night.

The next morning, after calling his dad, Randy Brazeal turned himself in to the police, claiming Richard Stokley had forced him to go along while Stokley attacked Mandy and Mary. After his arrest later that day, Stokley claimed Brazeal also took part in the raping and killing of the girls. A classic case of I didn't do it, he did. Evidence on the two suspects from one of the girls was gathered from Brazeal's car; however, DNA was then a relatively new science and was to play a major factor in the court case.

Deoxyribonucleic Acid (DNA) profiling to identify the matching DNA of an individual, such as a perpetrator in a crime was developed in 1984 by British Geneticist Sir Alec Jeffreys. The procedure was first used in forensic science to convict Colin Pitchfork a British convicted murderer and rapist. He was the first person convicted of a crime based on DNA evidence, and the first to be caught as a result of mass DNA screening. Pitchfork had raped and murdered two girls and was arrested in September 1987 and sentenced to life imprisonment on January 22, 1988, after admitting both murders. DNA was a major factor here in the Stokley/Brazeal Case eight years later even as profiling was still a relatively new science. At that time DNA generally required months to process.

In January, 2014, the author interviewed retired Coshise County Superior Court Judge Matthew Borowiec, who was the Presiding Judge in the case for both men. The Judge stated, "I didn't have a feeling that one was less culpable than the other." The judge acknowledged however that Brazeal's attorney refused the popular 'waiving time' variable. Since DNA testing was rather new, it was possible that it could take months to process the DNA evidence and thus not be back in time for the trial.

As such, Randy Brazeal requested to exercise his right to a speedy trial. Brazeal was sentenced to two concurrent terms of 20 years after being allowed to plead guilty to second-degree murder. Since he had invoked his right to a speedy trial, prosecutors said they offered him a plea agreement for fear they would not have the DNA evidence back from the lab before his trial date. His trial was set for October 22, 1991, and the DNA results were not expected back from the laboratory until late November. Completely opposite, Stokley's attorney waived the constitutional time limit set for a speedy trial, and although the other's attorney filed a motion for a continuance to wait for DNA results, for reasons unknown, no such continuance was granted. The deputy Cochise County attorney, Chris Roll who was supposed to try the case, believes that it was withdrawn. Rather than risk an acquittal fearing that Brazeal might get off completely due to the possibility that DNA results would not be returned in time for the trial, the Cochise County Attorney's office agreed to a plea deal. In that deal, 19-year-old Randy Brazeal admitted to two counts of second-degree murder and accepted a sentence of twenty years.

When the DNA results finally did come back, Chief Deputy Rodney Rothrock of the Arizona Cochise County Sheriff's office, the lead detective on the case, disclosed that according to the DNA results, both men were guilty. Lab work disclosed that Randy Brazeal had definitely been involved since the DNA indicated that Mandy's blood was in Brazeal's underwear and that DNA links to both Brazeal and Stokley were found in a vaginal swab.

Even though the deal had been sealed before Stokley's trial, DNA tests on semen retrieved from Mandy Meyers showed that both men had indeed raped her. The results helped seal Stokley's conviction, even though it and other forensic evidence around the scene also tended to buttress Stokley's 'equal partners in the crime' story to the detriment of Brazeal's version.

Patty Hancock, the mother of Mandy Meyers, had pushed for Brazeal to be committed as a sexually violent predator and the Department of Corrections ordered an evaluation under Arizona Revised Statute 36-3702(B). As Brazeal refused to take part in the process, the initial evaluation was completely based solely on his case and record. The County Attorney Ed Rheinheimer said "It is not automatically enough to determine that someone continues to be a sexually violent person just because he committed a sexually violent act at some point in the past". As such, the Arizona Department of Corrections sent a letter notifying the Cochise County Attorney's office that the psychologist who made the initial evaluation did not find enough evidence to warrant a second evaluation. This meant that the civil commitment process could not move forward and Brazeal's release on July 2, 2011 was guaranteed.

 Several months after Brazeal's plea deal, Richard Stokley's trial started on March 12, 1992 and the verdict came in on March 27, 1992. Stokley was found guilty of first-degree murder (not second-degree murder as Brazeal pleaded to) and was also found guilty of kidnapping and rape. Stokley was sentenced to death on July 14, 1992 due to three aggravating circumstances:

1. Especially heinous, cruel and depraved
2. Multiple murders and,
3. Age of victims (under 15).

The U.S. Supreme Court rulings cleared the way for the lethal injection given to Stokley after it denied two appeals on his behalf and declined without comment to block his execution. In his final appeals, Stokley's lawyers argued that he was entitled to a new hearing on sentencing evidence; they also said that his constitutional rights were violated because Brazeal was free after serving 20 years in prison. However, prosecutors defended disparity in sentences by saying that Brazeal negotiated a plea agreement.

Richard Stokley was executed 21 years later on December 4, 2013 at age 60 at the Florence Arizona Prison, having been convicted of murdering Mandy Meyers and Mary Snyder in 1991. The execution team had difficulty setting the two lines required and had to cut into the femoral vein in his leg. Before his execution, Stokley expressed regret but didn't apologize, and according to Paul Davenport, a journalist, stated: "I do wish that I could die doing something meaningful, you know, this seems like such a waste".

"He was a coward from the beginning and he died a coward," said Patty Hancock, the mother of one of the girls. "He never looked at us." Randy Brazeal, his partner in crime, was a free man having served his sentence at the time of Stokley's execution.

Looking at this case, it is evident that the judgement is not a completely flawless one, and this begs the question of whether the judicial system, saddled with the responsibility of hearing cases, examining the circumstances and evidence brought forth and finally sentencing the 'criminals,' can be completely trusted enough in the discharge of its duties- in this case, handing out of death sentences. Both men were guilty, as later revealed by the DNA results. Why then did one get the death sentence and the other, a prison term of twenty years and was alive and free when the other was put to death?

If we assume that it was because Brazeal negotiated a plea agreement while Stokley waived the constitutional time limit set for a speedy trial, then does that mean that the use of capital punishment is not based on the gravity of the offence committed but rather on how smart and calculative the defending lawyers of the *culprits* are? Even after it was evident that Stokley's account of Brazeal's involvement in the case was the correct version, and considering his insistence on a speedy trial, why then were Stokley's appeals turned down and was later executed while the partner was a free man on the streets? Is capital punishment then based on the sincerity of the judicial system in truly taking retribution on behalf of victims or simply on the intuition or free will of the prosecuting counsels and jury? This remains a question yet unanswered.

Stokley's execution was Arizona's 34th since 1992. The U.S. Supreme Court rulings cleared the way for the lethal injection given to Stokley after it denied two appeals on his behalf and declined without comment to block his execution. In his final appeals, Stokley's lawyers argued he was entitled to a new hearing on sentencing evidence. They also said his constitutional rights were violated because Brazeal was free after serving 20 years in prison. However, prosecutors defended the disparity in sentences by saying that Brazeal negotiated a plea agreement. According to Arizona Journalist Michael Kiefer, "They presented the plea deal as if there wasn't much alternative".

In the author's 2014 interview with Presiding Coshise County Superior Court Judge Matthew Borowiec, the Judge spoke about the period from conviction to execution:

"A jury finds a defendant guilty beyond a reasonable doubt based on evidence presented at a trial. Often, that is not all the evidence: there may be evidence excluded by our criminal rules and laws; evidence legally withheld illegally, or more often evidence not discovered until a later time. If society could be absolutely certain of a person's guilt, by the use of some infallible instrument or test, perhaps the death penalty would be imposed much sooner. But of course, there is no such instrument or test that is infallible. So, in many cases though the jury found guilt beyond a reasonable doubt, there is a societal lingering doubt. Hence the delays, petitions, appeals, first to ensure that the defendant had a fair trial, e.g., that only admissible evidence was presented and the totality of it, and second, to determine by some extraneous and perhaps subjective test whether in a particular case, the punishment fits the crime."

THE AMERICAN COURTS

The death penalty is described in The American Psychological Association (APA) Judicial Notebook by Drs. Ryan Winter and Jonathan Vallano in which they report recent death penalty findings in a 2015 Gallup poll. The disclosures indicate support for the death penalty in the United States is at a 40-year low, with a 63 percent favorability rating, which is a stark contrast to the 80 percent in the 1990s. Comparing state executed death to life in prison, the death favorability drops to 42 percent where it is also reflected in the number of death verdicts, as they have dropped with only 73 defendants sentenced to death and 35 executed in 2014. Contrast that figure with 279 sentences and 98 executions in 1999. Of the 32 death penalty states, only seven carried out executions in 2014, the fewest in 25 years. Further, eight states have abolished the death penalty since 2007, and no states have added the penalty. These statistics beg the questions: Do we still need the death penalty, does the public want the death penalty to continue, and is the death penalty doomed to die itself?

The Supreme Court of the United States, referred to as 'the court of last resort,' is the High Court in the United States Judicial System. It seems fitting then to disclose death penalty statements made by this high court as we examine the words of Associated Justices who sit in review of our actions relative to both judicial law and moralistic thoughts on the issue of the death penalty or 'state execution'.

Recently deceased Associated Justice Anthony Scalia (1936-2016), a considered conservative' jurist, in a May 2002 *First Things* article titled "God's Justice and Ours," (procon.org) wrote:

While my views on the morality of the death penalty have nothing to do with how I vote as a judge, they have a lot to do with whether I can or should be a judge at all. To put the point in the blunt terms employed by Justice Harold Blackmun towards the end of his career on the bench, when I sit on a Court that reviews and affirms capital convictions, I am part of 'the machinery of death.' My vote, when joined with at least four others, is, in most cases, the last step that permits an execution to proceed. I could not take part in that process if I believed what was being done to be immoral... In my view, the choice for the judge who believes the death penalty to be immoral is resignation, rather than simply ignoring duly enacted, constitutional laws and sabotaging death penalty cases. He has, after all, taken an oath to apply the laws and has been given no power to supplant them with rules of his own. Of course, if he feels strongly enough he can go beyond mere resignation and lead a political campaign to abolish the death penalty-and if that fails, lead a revolution. But rewrite the laws he cannot do.

Conversely, Justice Thurgood Marshall (1908-1993, the first African-American Justice and considered liberal jurist some 30 years earlier in a 1972 concurrent opinion in Furman v. Georgia, 408 U.S. 238 1972, wrote:

[Capital punishment] violates the Eighth Amendment because it is morally unacceptable to the people of the United States at this time in their history. In judging whether or not a given penalty is morally acceptable, most courts have said that the punishment is valid unless 'it shocks the conscience and sense of justice of the people.' Assuming knowledge of all the facts presently available regarding capital punishment, the average citizen would, in my opinion, find it shocking to his conscience and sense of justice. For this reason alone, capital punishment cannot stand."

Note: *Furman v. Georgia*, 408 U.S. 238 (1972) was the criminal case in which the United States Supreme Court struck down all death penalty schemes in the United States in a 5–4 decision, with each member of the majority writing a separate opinion. Following *Furman*, in order to reinstate the death penalty, states had to at least remove arbitrary and discriminatory effects, to satisfy the Eighth Amendment to the United States Constitution.

The decision ruled on the requirement for a degree of consistency in the application of the death penalty. This case led to a *de facto* moratorium on capital punishment throughout the United States, which came to an end when *Gregg v. Georgia* was decided in 1976 to allow the death penalty.

Examining the changing views of our Supreme Court Justices, we find the following. In his article 'Repudiating Death,' William Berry writes in the *Journal of Criminal Law and Criminology*:

In recent years, three Supreme Court Justices, Powell, Blackmun, and Stevens, have all called for the abolition of the death penalty, repudiating their prior approval of the use of capital punishment. The Article conceptualizes these reversals not as normative shifts on the morality of capital punishment, but instead as shifts in the Justices' views concerning their own need to exercise judicial restraint towards the states with respect to the death penalty. Two separate decisions comprise their abandonment of judicial restraint. First, Justices Powell, Blackmun, and Stevens all acquiesce to the decision of the Court to use the Eighth Amendment to regulate the states' administration of capital punishment. Later, each of the three Justices separately advocates interpreting the Eighth Amendment to prohibit the states' use of the death penalty entirely. The journal article argues that both of these decisions to abandon deference to the states reflect, on the part of Justices Powell, Blackmun, and Stevens, a diminishing view of the Court's duty to exercise judicial restraint with respect to state legislatures and their use of the death penalty. In addition to explaining why their respective rejections of the death penalty were institutional (and not moral) choices, the article argues that these repudiations were the inevitable consequence of the initial decision to use the Eighth Amendment to regulate the death penalty. The experience of these Justices and the Court over the past thirty-five years demonstrates the extreme difficulty in interpreting and applying the Eighth Amendment in a manner that ensures that states' administration of the death penalty is fair and non-arbitrary. When one premises his support of capital punishment upon the notion that the application of the Eighth Amendment can achieve these goals, as Justices Powell, Blackmun, and Stevens did, the futility of trying to correct the myriad of problems with the states' use of the death penalty leads to the conclusion that no fruitful remedy exists other than abolishing capital punishment.

The Supreme Court has ruled that the death penalty is not a violation of the Eighth Amendment's ban on cruel and unusual punishment per se, but the Eighth Amendment does shape certain procedural aspects regarding when a jury may use the death penalty and how it must be carried out. The number of executions in the United States has fallen in 14 of the last 19 years, from a high of 98 in 1999. After reaching a 14-year low in 2008, executions increased by 15 in 2009 before declining or remaining steady for the next seven years.

As of this writing, Alabama's execution of Cop Killer Torrey McNabb on October 19, 2017 for the 1997 murder of Montgomery Police Cpl. Anderson Gordon III was the 21st execution in the United States in 2017, with seven more executions scheduled. If all are carried out, the number of executions over the last three years will still fall by seven, with an average of 25.3 executions per year; there will be a decrease of 15 executions over the past five years, with the average number of executions over that period falling to 30.4 per year; and there will be a decrease of 14 executions over the past decade, with the average number of executions per year falling to 37.1.

According to an analysis by The Marshall Project, a nonpartisan, non-profit news organization that seeks to create and sustain a sense of national urgency about the U.S. criminal justice system, the increase in the number of executions in 2017 "does not suggest that executions are likely to become more common." Instead, it reports, "executions are likely to keep declining for one big reason: juries are handing out fewer death sentences." *USA Today* reports that the executions today are the remnants of "largely decades-old death sentences being carried out." Those executions, the paper reports, "have illustrated the problems [death-penalty] opponents highlight in their quest to end capital punishment," including unaddressed claims of innocence and requests for forensic testing, lack of transparency in carrying out executions, and race-of-victim disparities—"nearly all the murder victims [in the execution cases] were white."

Rob Smith, executive director of the Fair Punishment Project, said that the people being executed today were sentenced years ago "by juries who would never return that death sentence today and prosecutors who would never seek that death sentence today." He said the historic decline in new death sentences, from more than 300 per year in the mid-1990s to fewer than 50 per year, will result in fewer executions going forward.

Heather Beaudoin, national organizer for death-penalty abolitionist group, Equal Justice USA, said she is "not discourage[d]" by this year's execution numbers. What "we're seeing [is] the last grasps of trying to hold on to the death penalty in this country."

Ben Cohen, a lawyer with the Capital Appeals Project in New Orleans, said today's executions largely involve cases tried "twenty years ago [during] the height of the death sentencing era." The "long-term trend," he told *USA Today*, "remains clearly aimed at replacing death sentences and executions with life without parole."

Over the years, there has been an increase in the debate on whether the death penalty is the best form of punishment that can and should be meted out on offenders who commit capital crimes. While some have argued that it is morally wrong to kill someone in return for killing another, others strongly believe that it is the best way of deterrence as death makes a lasting impression on intending offenders.

Society and even religious sects have become divided on the issue of capital punishment, with some insisting that it has done more good than harm in the maintenance of law and order and some insisting it is only doubling the number of criminals: the initial offender and the person who ends up placing a death sentence on him. Some have asked if capital punishment is truly a fair branch in justice, why then is it that the offences carrying the death penalty differ from one country to another (as discussed later in this book)? It is mainly murder cases that attract the death penalty in the U.S. while a lesser crime such as sabotaging social amenities like electricity or pipe borne water attracts the same penalty in China.

Others have demanded an explanation for some people unfortunate enough to have been executed for crimes later found out to have been committed by others, or the fact that the life that we highly claim to cherish and preserve is now to be taken in retribution of an offence committed. Can we even say that the justice system is fair enough in its discharge? Or that the many offences tagged as warranting the death penalty are really worth taking lives for, not to mention the fact that some of these sentences are based on the judge's belief or frame of mind at the time of pronouncing the judgement on the 'accused'?

In view of the controversies surrounding the death penalty as a form of punishment for offences considered 'capital', we might want to focus our aims at unravelling the numerous conflicting opinions. Extensively discussing the terms on the topics of morality, capital offences and punishments; their various supporting views on the death penalty with counteracting opinions on the death penalty; effects of the death penalty on crime rates in countries upholding them; the various forms of carrying out the execution with emphasis on the use of lethal injection in the U.S., These thoughts merits cases attracting the death penalty and the conclusion on how the death penalty portrays us as a society with good moral values and of course the morality of totality.

MORALITY

Morality can be defined as the differentiation of intentions, decisions and actions between those that are distinguished as proper and those that are improper. It can be a body of standards of principles derived from a code of conduct from a particular philosophy, religion or culture, or it can be derived from a standard that a person believes should be universal.

The words 'morals' and 'ethics are often used interchangeably but a useful distinction can be made between both terms: Morality is the system through which we determine right and wrong conduct, i.e. the guide to good or bad behaviour, while ethics is said to be the philosophical study of morality.

In its descriptive sense, morality refers to personal or cultural values, codes of conduct or social mores from a society that provides these codes of conduct in which it applies and is accepted by an individual. It does not connote objective claims of right or wrong, but only refers to that which is considered right or wrong.

Morality in the normative sense refers to whatever is actually right or wrong, which may be independent of the values or morals held by any particular people or culture. The development of modern morality is the process closely tied to socio-cultural evolution and is believed to be a product of evolutionary forces acting at both the individual and group level. Marc Bekoff and Jessica Pierce (2009) define morality as a suite of interrelated behaviours that cultivate and regulate complex interactions between socio groups.

It is noteworthy that the concept of morality is viewed differently by different people and sects, but according to Gregory E. Ganssle in his book *Thinking about God: First steps in Philosophy,* there are five particular views pertaining to morality and as one examines these views, it becomes clear that one view of morality stands above and beyond the value of the other moral opinions. These views are:

The Error Theory

Holds that there are no moral facts, that it is factually wrong to claim any form of morality. This theory, while held by some philosophers, could be attributed to some Eastern religions which claim that good and evil are just illusions and aren't real.

Objective Morality: This theory views morality as transcendent reality which applies to all individuals and society, i.e. moral absolutes are unavoidable even if our understanding of them or the circumstances in which they should be applied are not. An objective moral is held by all people. While different tribes and societies hold different outlooks on other matters of morality, the core morals are the same - *It is wrong to murder. It is wrong to steal. It is wrong to commit adultery.*

The Evolutionary Theory:

Views falling in line with Charles Darwin's "survival of the fittest" philosophy. It is held that treating other people in good ways rather than bad helped the human species to survive.

Cultural Relativism: Cultural relativists claim that morality is set by the cultural undertone of an area. That is, "What is right or wrong is determined by one's culture or society". This theory believes that we cannot criticize the actions of those in cultures other than our own and this fact might amount to the denial of a universal set of moral principles. *You are only wrong if you are practice our culture and we all believe it's wrong.*

Individual Relativism

Explained by the classic phrase, "What is good for you may not be good for me". That is, individual relativism is the belief that the individual sets forth his or her own morality and so each person must decide what is good or bad themselves

In a bid to effectively define what morals are, other entities have developed some theories on how to aptly describe morality. These are:

Moral Subjectivism: Amounts to the denial of moral principles of any significant kind, and the possibility of moral criticism and argumentation. What this theory believes is that what you consider right or wrong is determined by no other person or institution but you, as the subject. If I feel that stealing is right and another person thinks it is wrong, then as moral subjectivists, we do not need to refute each other's claim because we are both right and neither is wrong.

Ethical Egoism: Theory holds that right and wrong is determined by what is in your self-interest. An ethical egoist will claim that the altruist helps others only because they want to derive pleasure out of helping others or because they think there will be some personal advantage in doing so. *This is wrong because it is not in my interest and this is right as long as it is for my good.*

Divine Command Theory: Claims there is a necessary connection between morality and religion, such that without religion, there is no right and wrong behaviour. The upshot of this theory is that an action is right or obligatory if God commands that we do it, wrong if God commands that we refrain from doing it, and morally permissible if God does not command that it should not be done. *It is wrong to kill because God commands us to uphold life, and right to help others because God commands that we do good always.*

Utilitarianism: Right and wrong is determined by the overall goodness (utility) of the consequences of the action. We decide on which action is right or wrong by considering the maximum pleasure or happiness that we get and the suffering that we minimize by doing it. For Utilitarians, no action is intrinsically right or wrong, and no person's preferences or interests carry a greater weight than any other person's. So, in general, morally right actions are those that produce the best overall consequences and total amount of pleasure or absence of pain.

Kantian Theory: Upholds that good and evil are defined in terms of law, duty and obligation, i.e. right and wrong is determined by rationality and giving universal duties. The theory believes that actions are truly moral only if they have the right intention, i.e. are based on goodwill.

Contractarianism: Believes that the principles of right and wrong or justice are those which everyone in society would agree upon in forming a social contract. Various forms of contractarianism have been suggested and the general idea is that the principle or rules that determine right and wrong in society are determined by a hypothetical contract which forms proc

Virtue Ethics: Proposes that right and wrong are characterised in terms of acting in accordance with the traditional virtues - making a good person. There are 3 steps.

The ultimate end of human action is happiness

Happiness consists of acting in accordance with reason. Acting in accordance with reason is the distinguishing feature of all the traditional virtues.

They believe that humans have a specific function, and this is to lead a life of true flourishing as a human. This requires abiding by the dictates of rationality and so acting in accordance with traditional virtues.

Another division not entirely as prominent as the aforementioned ones is that of the Buddhists, who believe that there are three types of moral discipline: *personal morality or individual liberation where morality motivated by cherishing others* and *tantric morality (ultimate self-awareness):*

Personal Morality: Dwells on looking at one's personal actions. It is a theory that is considered very present and practical. Some of the questions that can be asked under this theory include: What causes real inner happiness? How will refraining from certain actions bring peace to myself? What can I do to protect myself from the suffering of my future?

Bodhisattva Morality: This is also known as the morality that is motivated by cherishing others. The major belief of this theory is that if one cannot help others, then one should at least refrain from harming others. They ask questions like: How can I help people attain the same enlightened state that I wish for? How can release myself from self-cherishing to help me help them? Do I recognise how my selfish attitude affects others?

Tantric Morality or the ultimate self-awareness theory hinges on changing how I see myself and others, creating a new world for myself and others.

CAPITAL OFFENCES

The legal definition of capital offences is anoffence for which the punishment or one of the punishments is death. Capital offences vary from one country to another, as what is considered 'capital' in one might not warrant the death penalty in another.

We should also note that despite the worldwide call for lesser and more humane forms of punishment for criminals, some countries have insisted on the death penalty as the ultimate form of punishment for offences they consider worthy. Some of these countries are reviewed below.

In the U.S., the federal government lists 41 capital offences which include espionage, treason and death resulting from aircraft hijacking. These offences also include various forms of murder such as those committed during a drug-related drive-by shooting, murder during a kidnapping, murder related to rape or child molestation, murder involving torture, murder for hire, murder of a member of congress, an important executive official, or a supreme court justice, murder committed by the use of firearm during a crime or violence, murder committed in a federal government facility, first-degree murder, murder by a federal prisoner, murder of a state or local law enforcement official, retaliatory murder of a witness, victim or informant, murder relating to the smuggling of aliens, retaliatory murder of a member of the immediate family of law enforcement officials, civil right offences resulting in death, murder of a foreign official, murder by a federal prisoner, murder of a court officer or juror, mailing of injurious articles with intent to kill or resulting in death, bank-robbery-related murder or kidnapping, murder related to carjacking, murder by the use of a weapon of mass destruction, genocide, etc.

India

Provides 12 major offences punishable by death. These are: waging or attempting to wage war against the government of India, abetting a mutiny in the armed forces, giving or fabricating false evidence with intent to procure a conviction of a capital offence, murder, abetting the suicide of a minor, aiding or abetting an act of Sati (the act of burying alive or burning a woman alongside her deceased husband or relative), kidnapping in the cause of which the victim was held for ransom or other coercive purposes, drug trafficking in cases of repeat offences, banditry with murder (if a member of a team of bandits of five or more kills anyone, then all the members of that group are liable to receive the death sentence), rape if the perpetrator inflicts injuries that result in the victim's death or incapacitation in a persistent vegetative state or is a repeat offender, manufacturing and sale of poisoned alcohol which results in death (in Gujarat only) and being a party to a criminal conspiracy to commit a capital offence.

In India, originally detained in 1996, Renuka Shinde, 41, and 36-year-old Seema Gavit were convicted of kidnapping and killing five children in 2001. In 2004, an appeal court upheld their death sentence of hanging and two years later India's Supreme Court did the same. In April 2017, the sisters stated that they shouldn't be hanged on the gallows as doing so would more "barbaric" than they deserve. The sisters are now among 13 women on death row in India, including Fahmida Sayed, who planted a car bomb in Mumbai that left 54 people dead in 2003. The last woman to be hanged in the country was in 1955.

Nigeria Africa,

Capital punishment is legal and in 2016, three executions were carried out, the first since 2013. In 2017, the Nigerian government rejected the call by Amnesty International to halt the planned execution of some inmates on death row in Lagos State, and pointed that the death penalty was expressly authorized by section 33 of the Constitution of Nigeria. Five offences are punishable by death: murder, treason, treachery, directing and controlling or presiding at an unlawful trial by ordeal from which death results and conviction for armed robbery. However, a crime like adultery attracts the death penalty in some states like Zamfara which practices the Shariah law.

China

Provides 46 criminal offences that are eligible for the death penalty, many of which are non-violent and economic criminal offences. As of June 2016, sixty-eight different crimes - more than half non-violent offences such as tax evasion and drug smuggling - are punishable by death in the country. Some of these other capital offences include treason, providing material support to the enemy, armed rebellion or rioting, arson, flooding, bombing, hijacking aircraft, theft of firearms, ammunition or other dangerous materials, production or sale of counterfeit medicine, intentional homicide and assault, rape, kidnapping and human trafficking, robbery, embezzlement, insubordination, prison escape or jail break, refusing to pass or falsely passing orders (military), cowardice, etc. As of April, 2014, according to the Dui Hua Foundation, lethal injection and shooting are the only methods authorized by the People's Republic of China for China's Criminal Procedure Law of 1996. According to *Reuters News* and *CNN* (2009), some Chinese provinces are projected to end shooting executions and swap bullets for lethal injections in part due to family complaints of massive disfiguration caused by shots to the back of the head.

Saudi Arabia

Capital punishment is a legal penalty and in 2016 the country performed at least 154 executions, while in 2015 158 people were executed. The death penalty is theoretically allowed for crimes such as treason, espionage, murder, rape, terrorism, drug smuggling, armed robbery, apostasy, atheism, social misconduct, sodomy, homosexuality or lesbianism, sorcery and witchcraft, blaspheming, etc.

Israel,

Capital punishment is extremely rare and allowed only during war time and only for genocide, crimes against humanity, war crimes, crimes against the Jewish people, treason, and certain crimes under military law. The rare use of the death penalty may be partly due to Jewish religious law, because since the beginning of the common era Jewish scholars developed such restrictive rules to prevent executing the innocent, thus the death penalty has become de facto abolished. The last execution was carried out in 1962 when Holocaust architect Adolf Eichmann was hanged for genocide and crimes against humanity, and the last death sentence in the country was handed down in 1988 and was subsequently overturned. No death sentences have been sought by Israeli prosecutors since the 1990s.

CAPITAL PUNISHMENT

Before defining the term 'capital punishment', it is expedient to first define what punishment is and the reason for meting out punishment on offenders. According to James Fieser in *Moral Issues that Divide Us*, "a basic definition of punishment is that it involves the deliberate infliction of suffering on a supposed or actual offender for an offence such as a moral or legal transgression." Fieser posits further that all forms of punishment have some aim which serves to justify the suffering that is inflicted on the offender. The main aims are retribution, incapacitation, rehabilitation and deterrence.

Retribution

Punishment is most often associated with the notion of "eye for an eye" justice, where punishment is a matter of what is deserved in return for a wrongful act, i.e. the imposed punishment is equal to the harm done. Sometimes the "eye for an eye" concept of punishment is taken literally, such as the following from the ancient Babylonian *Law of Hammurabi* (c. 1750 BCE): "If a man puts out the eye of another man, then his eye shall be put out. If he breaks another man's bone, then his bone shall be broken." The concept is probably most known from its appearance in the Hebrew Bible, that "Anyone who injures their neighbour is to be injured in the same manner: fracture for fracture, eye for eye, tooth for tooth. The one who has inflicted the injury must suffer the same injury" (Leviticus. 24:19–21).

Incapacitation

Believes punishment keeps offenders from repeating the same crimes, typically by physically restraining them. When we catch violent criminals, one of our first thought is to get them off the street before they harm others.

With rehabilitation, punishment aims to change the offender's predisposition towards criminal behaviour and thus keeps him from becoming a threat to others when released into the community. This is sometimes facilitated through psychological counselling or other types of behaviour-modification therapy. However, the assumption here is that any type of punishment, if it is memorable enough, will in and of itself discourage criminals from repeating crimes. With deterrence, punishment is a means of discouraging others from committing similar offences. The aim here is to use the criminal as an example from which others can learn.

Another infrequently discussed aim of punishment that will be difficult to discard is the concept of revenge which involves doing something out of anger or resentment as a retaliatory measure. This means that one has the opportunity to vent one's rage and get some sense of satisfaction and closure from one's ordeal when the perpetrator has been harshly punished. What distinguishes revenge from retributive aims of punishment is impartiality. Revenge stems from an individual's personal desire for retaliation, whereas retribution considers more abstractly what justice calls for in a specific situation.

Having discussed the concept of punishment and its aims, one can then move ahead to explain what capital punishment deals with. Capital punishment, also known as the *"death penalty,"* is a government sanctioned practice whereby the person is put to death by the state as the punishment for a crime committed. The sentence where someone will be punished in such a manner is referred to as a death sentence, whereas the act of carrying out the sentence is known as an execution.

Capital punishment is a matter of active controversy in various countries and states, and positions can vary within a single political ideology or cultural region. Although most nations have abolished capital punishment, over 60% of the world's population lives in countries where execution takes place such as China, the United States, India, and Indonesia.

Execution of criminals has been used by nearly all societies, as it has been a common practice around the world as far back as historical records, and it is easy to imagine primitive social environments in which citizens would have no choice but to kill criminals. Until the 19th century, without developed prison systems, there were frequently no workable alternatives to ensure deterrence and incapacitation of criminals. Forms of execution in those days included strangulation, decapitation, slow slicing - also known as Ling Chi or death by a thousand cuts - scourging to death with a thick rod, truncation - the convicted person was cut into 2 at the waist with a fodder knife and then left to bleed to death - the breaking wheel method and burning.

In the modern day, there has been a movement towards non-painful execution: France developed guillotine in the final year of the 18th century; Britain replaced hanging by turning the victim off a ladder or kicking a stool using the drop from a longer distance to dislocate the neck and sever the spinal cord rather than slowly suffocating the individual.

Persia introduced throat-cutting and blowing from as quick and painless alternatives to more torturous methods of execution used at that time while the U.S. introduced electrocution, gas inhalation, and recently lethal injection as more humane options.

The following methods of execution were used in 2015:
Hanging (Afghanistan, Iran, Iraq, Egypt, Liberia, Malawi, Yemen, Palestine, Japan, Zimbabwe, India, Chad, Washington State in the USA).
Shooting (The People's Republic of China, North Korea, Vietnam, Belarus, Indonesia, Yemen and in the U.S. states of Oklahoma and Utah).
Lethal injection (US Thailand, Vietnam, Guatemala, and the People's Republic of China).
Electrocution and gas (If requested in some US S. states if lethal injection is not available).
Beheading (Saudi Arabia).

Another form of capital punishment is public execution, in which members of the general public may voluntarily attend. While the great majority of the world considers public execution to be distasteful today and most countries have banned the practice, many executions throughout history were performed publicly as a means for the state to demonstrate its power and the public a chance to witness what was considered "a great spectacle". According to Amnesty International, public executions were known to have been carried out in Iran, North Korea, Saudi Arabia and Somalia in 2012. There have also been reports of public execution carried out by state and non-state actors in Syria, Afghanistan and Yemen while executions which can be classified as public were also carried out in the U.S. states of Florida and Utah as of 1992.

THE ABOLITIONIST AND RETENTIONIST COUNTRIES

Capital punishment, also known as the death penalty as earlier explained, is a topic that has called for major deliberations over the years. International organizations and civil rights groups have clamored for the total abolition of the death penalty for any offence committed and have given other options like life imprisonment as replacement.

Abolition was often adopted due to political change, as when countries shifted from authoritarianism to democracy, or when it became an entry condition for the European Union.

While some countries have heeded the call, and have either abolished the punishment completely, partly for some crimes or stalled executions for years, there are still some who have insisted on continuing the act, stating it is the best form of punishment they know. Below are the statistics released by Amnesty International as of the 31st of December, 2016.

Abolitionist for all crimes - These are countries whose laws do not provide for the death penalty for any crime. There are 104 countries practicing this, and among them are Mexico, Argentina, Armenia, Australia, Belgium, Burundi, Canada, People's Republic of Congo, Denmark, Finland, France, Gabon, New Zealand, Madagascar, Mozambique, Namibia, Georgia, Germany, Greece, Haiti, Italy, Luxembourg, Senegal, Paraguay, Norway, Ukraine, Togo, Turkey, and Venezuela.

Abolitionist for 'ordinary crimes' only - These are countries whose laws provide for the death penalty only for exceptional crimes or crimes committed in exceptional circumstances. There are 7 countries in this category: Brazil, Chile, El Salvador, Guinea, Israel, Peru and Kazakhstan.

Abolitionist in practice - These are countries which retain the death penalty for ordinary crimes such as murder but can be abolitionist in practice, in that they have not executed anyone during the past 10 years and have a policy or established practice of not carrying out executions. The list also includes countries that have made an international commitment not to use the death penalty. There are 30 countries in all and they include Algeria, Burkina Faso, Cameroon, Central African Republic, Ghana, Kenya, South Korea, Liberia, Malawi, Mali, Mongolia, Morocco, Niger, Tanzania, Sri Lanka, and Zambia.

COUNTRIES THAT HAVE ABOLISHED THE DEATH PENALTY SINCE 1976.

1976 - Portugal abolished the death penalty for all crimes.

1978 - Denmark abolished the death penalty for all crimes.

1979 - Luxembourg, Nicaragua and Norway abolished the death penalty for all crimes

1979- Peru abolished the death penalty for ordinary crimes.

1981 - France and Cape Verde abolished the death penalty for all crimes.

1982 - The Netherlands abolished the death penalty for all crimes.

1983 - Cyprus and El Salvador abolished the death penalty for ordinary crimes.

1984 - Argentina abolished the death penalty for ordinary crimes.

1985- Australia abolished the death penalty for all crimes.

1987-   Haiti, Liechtenstein and the German Democratic Republic abolished the death penalty.

1989-   Cambodia, New Zealand, Romania and Slovenia abolished the death penalty

1990-   Andorra, Croatia, the Czech and Slovak Republic, Hungary, Mozambique, Namibia

1990-   Sao Tome and Principe abolished the death penalty for all crimes.

1992-   Angola, Paraguay, and Switzerland abolished the death penalty for all crimes.

1993-   Guinea-Bissau, Hong Kong and Seychelles for ordinary crimes.

1994-   Italy abolished the death penalty for all crimes.

1995-   Djibouti, Mauritius, Moldova and Spain abolished the death penalty for all crimes.

1996-   Belgium abolished the death penalty for all crimes.

1997-   Georgia, Nepal, Poland and South Africa abolished the death penalty for all crimes

1997-   Bosnia-Herzegovina abolished the death penalty for ordinary crimes.

1998-   Azerbaijan, Bulgaria, Canada, Estonia, Lithuania and the United Kingdom

1999-   East Timor, Turkmenistan and Ukraine abolished the death penalty for all crimes.

2000-   Cote D'ivoire and Malta abolished the death penalty for all crimes while

2000-   Albania abolished the death penalty for ordinary crimes.

2001-   Bosnia-Herzegovina abolished the death penalty for all crimes

2001-   Chile abolished the death penalty for ordinary crimes.

2002-   Turkey abolished the death penalty for ordinary crimes

2002-   Serbia, Montenegro and Cyprus abolished the death penalty for all crimes.

2003-   Armenia abolished the death penalty for ordinary crimes.

2004- Bhutan, Samoa, Senegal and Turkey abolished the death penalty for all crimes.

2005- Liberia and Mexico abolished the death penalty for all crimes.

2006- The Philippines abolished the death penalty for all crimes.

2007- Albania and Rwanda abolished the death penalty for all crimes

2007- Kyrgyzstan abolished the death penalty for ordinary crimes.

2008- Uzbekistan, Chile and Argentina abolished the death penalty for all crimes.

2009- Burundi and Togo abolished the death penalty for all crimes.

2010- Gabon removed the death penalty from its legislation.

2012- Latvia abolished the death penalty for all crimes.

2013- Bolivia abolished the death penalty for all crimes.

2015-	Congo (Republic), Fiji, Madagascar and Suriname abolished the death penalty
2016-	Benin and Nauru abolished the death penalty for all crimes
2016-	Guinea abolished the death penalty for ordinary crimes.

RETENTIONIST COUNTRIES

In spite of the large number of countries that have seen reasons as to why the death penalty shouldn't be the only option available for heinous crimes, there are other countries that have retained this punishment. These countries are known as the retentionist countries because they have retained the death penalty for 'ordinary crimes.' The debate on the abolition of capital punishment is sometimes revived when a miscarriage of justice has occurred, though this tends to cause legislative efforts to improve the judicial process rather than abolish the death penalty. They are 57 of these countries and the list is as follows: Afghanistan, Antigua, Barbuda, Bahamas, Bahrain, Belarus, Barbados, Bangladesh, Belize, Botswana, Chad, China, Congo, Palestinian Authority, Comoros, Cuba, Egypt, Dominica, Equatorial, Guinea, Ethiopia, Gambi, Grenadines, Guatemala, Guyana, India, Indonesia, Iran, Iraq, Jamaica, North Korea, Japan, Jordan, Kuwait, Lebanon, Lesotho, Libya, Malaysia, Nigeria, Oman, Pakistan Qatar, Saint Kitts,

Saint Vincent, ,Saint Lucia, Saudi Arabia, Syria, Sudan, Syria, Taiwan, Trinidad and Tobago, Thailand, United Arab Emirates, Yemen, Zimbabwe, Uganda, and the United States of America. It is interesting to note that the modes of execution in all these retentionist countries vary from one to another and the crimes for which capital punishment is assigned also differ, depending on the instinct and laws of each country. These stated facts will be extensively treated in the course of this book.

RETENTIONIST COUNTRIES AND METHODS OF EXECUTION

This section will investigate death penalties in some of the countries still practicing it, their methods of execution and selected cases of people that have been executed. In this section, five countries have been randomly selected across the continents.

Asia-Pacific

Saudi Arabia and the Death Penalty

Capital punishment is a legal penalty in Saudi Arabia. Death sentences are pronounced almost exclusively based on the system of judicial sentencing discretion *Tazir* rather than Shariah-prescribed *Hu dud* punishment, following the classical principles that Hu dud penalties should be avoided if possible. The country has a criminal justice system based on a hard line and literal form of Shariah law reflecting a particular state-sanctioned interpretation of Islam. It is usually carried out publicly by beheading with a sword and occasionally performed by shooting.The

Saudi Judiciary can impose the death penalty according to 3 categories of criminal offence in Shariah law:

Hu dud - fixed Quranic punishment for specific crimes. Hu dud crimes which can result in the death penalty include apostasy, adultery and sodomy.

Qis as - eye-for-an-eye retaliatory punishments. Qis as crimes include murder, and in this case families of someone murdered can choose between demanding the death penalty or granting clemency in return for a payment of *diyya,* or blood money, by the perpetrator.

Tazir - a general category, including crimes defined by national regulations, some of which can be punished by death such as drug trafficking.

A conviction in Saudi Arabia requires proof in one of three ways:

An uncoerced confession.

The testimony of two male witnesses can result in conviction. This however excludes 'hudud crimes' in which case a confession is also required. An affirmation or denial by oath can be required. Giving an oath is particularly taken seriously in a religious society such as Saudi Arabia and a refusal to take an oath will be taken on an admission of guilt resulting in conviction.

On January 2, 2016, the kingdom of Saudi Arabia carried out a mass execution of 47 imprisoned civilians convicted for terrorism in 12 different provinces in the country. Forty-three (43) were beheaded and four (4) were executed by firing squads. The execution was the largest carried out in the Kingdom since 1980. In 2015, 158 people were executed by the Saudi authorities. The rise in death sentences during recent decades resulted from a concerted reaction by the government and the courts to a rise of violent crime in the 1970s and paralleled similar developments in the U.S. and China.

The use of public beheading as a method of capital punishment and the number of executions have attracted strong international criticism. Several executions, particularly of foreign workers, have also sparked international outcries. In June, 2011, Ruyati Binti Satubi, an Indonesia maid, was beheaded for killing her employer's wife reportedly after years of abuse, and this drew extensive criticism. September, 2011, saw the beheading of Sudanese migrant worker for sorcery, an execution which Amnesty International condemned as 'appalling'.

According to figures by Amnesty International, in 2010 at least 27 migrant workers were executed and as of January, 2013, more than 45 foreign maids were on death row and awaiting execution.

China and the Death Penalty

Capital punishment was one of the classical five punishments of China's dynastic period. During its early dynasties, capital punishment and amputation were predominant among the five punishments but amputation became less common later on while capital and corporal punishment remained. The number of types of capital offences also varied over time; there were 200 capital offences under Lu Xing (475 - 221 BCE), the Tang Code (653 CE) listed 233 capital offences and the Song Dynasty (960-1279) retained this and added 60 more over time. The Qing Dynasty (1644 - 1911) had the highest number of capital offences with more than 800.

By the confirmed numbers, the rate of execution in China is higher than the United States and Pakistan, though Iran executes more prisoners per capita. The Dui Hua foundation estimates that China executed 12,000 people in 2002, 6,500 in 2007 and roughly 2,400 in 2013 and 2014, i.e. execution in China accounts for more than 58% of the world-wide number of executions in 2009 and 65% in 2010.

The exact number of people executed in China is classified as a State secret; occasionally, death penalty cases are posted publicly by the Judiciary as in certain high-profile cases, e.g. the execution of former State Food and Drug Director Zheng Xiaoyu, which was confirmed by both State television and other media outlets.

China commonly employs two methods of execution. Since 1949, the most common method has been execution by firing squad, which has been largely superceded by lethal injection using the same 3-drug cocktail pioneered by the United States, introduced in 1996. Lethal injection is more commonly used for 'economic crimes' such as corruption while firing squads are used for more common crimes like murder. However, in 2010, the country moved to have lethal injection become the dominant form of execution in some provinces and municipalities, so it is now the only legal form of capital punishment.

Because of the wide application of capital offences in Chinese criminal law, substantial use of capital punishment, and the hidden execution rate, the Chinese death penalty system has been criticised by many international organisations from perspectives such as the right to live, presumption of innocence and proportionality. Human rights groups and foreign governments have also criticised China's use of the death penalty for a variety of reasons, including its application for non-violent offences, allegations of the use of torture to extract confessions, legal proceedings that do not meet international standards, and the government's refusal to publish statistics on the death penalty.

Africa

Nigeria and the Death Penalty

Capital punishment is a legal penalty in Nigeria that is provided for in section 33(1) of the Nigerian constitution. Specifically, the cited section states as follows:

"Every person has a right to life, and no one shall be deprived intentionally of his life save in execution of the sentence of a court in respect of a criminal offence of which one has been found guilty in Nigeria".

Methods of execution are:

Hanging - This is the method of execution under secular law and is also applied in some northern Nigerian states using the Shari'ah law. Death sentences can be carried out by hanging, if so decided by the Governor under the Federal Robbery and Fire Arms Act applicable in the Federal Capital Territory. However, the High Court of Lagos declared that execution by hanging is unconstitutional, but this ruling is only enforceable within Lagos State.

Shooting - Executions can be carried out by firing squad under the Shari'ah applied in some northern Nigerian states. If decided by the Governor, death sentences can be carried out by firing squad under the Federal Robbery and Fire Arms Act applicable in the Federal Capital Territory. Lagos State again is an exception from this rule.

Stoning - *Rajma* is a Shari'ah law punishment applied in some northern states and reserved for Muslims. The punishment applies broadly for adultery, rape (if the offender is married), incest (if the offender is married) and homosexual sodomy. It should be noted that evidentiary requirements for demonstrating these offences, if enforced, are very demanding.

Crucifixion - *Salb* is a form of punishment under Shari'ah for *Hirabah* (armed robbery) resulting in death when property is actually taken. However, Nigerian states still differ on what is meant by crucifixion.

Execution Ratio

2016 - Three executions were carried out secretly in Benin City

2014* -

2015: - 0

2013 - 4

2007 - 2012 - 0

* On 17 December, 2014, about 54 Nigerian soldiers were sentenced to death by firing squad after they were found guilty of mutiny.

In states applying Shari'ah law, practicing indigenous beliefs may be considered witchcraft and punished by death even when they are of little or no harm. Shari'ah rules of procedure establish that very high evidentiary requirements must be met before the death penalty can be applied to offences against sexual morals.

Categories of offenders excluded from death penalties are:
Individuals below age 18 at the time of crime: The Federal Child Act defines juveniles as children under the age of 18 and thus prohibits sentencing them to

capital punishments. This act, however, is only enforceable in Abuja and in states which have explicitly enacted it. Furthermore, under Shari'ah law applicable in at least 12 states, juveniles who committed offences after reaching puberty or 'the age of responsibility' can be executed. In 2010, there were 40 death row inmates believed to have been under the age of 18 at the time of their offences, and there have been no reports that these death sentences were reviewed.

In June, 2014, the ECOWAS Court of Justice issued a judgement holding that the death sentence of Maimuna Abdulmumini, who was convicted of murdering her husband at the age of 13, was a violation of the ICCPR's prohibition of applying capital punishment to minors. The Court then awarded Maimuna trial costs and damages.

Pregnant women: At the end of 2011, an estimated 16 women were on death row but facts did not reveal if any of them were pregnant or not. Under the Nigerian

Criminal Procedure Act, pregnant women cannot be sentenced to death and their sentences should be commuted to life imprisonment instead. However, Shari'ah penal laws in some states in Nigeria authorise the imposition of death penalties on pregnant women, but this practice seems to be out of line with observations of Shari'ah law outside of Nigeria which generally does not condone the execution of pregnant women.

Mentally ill: The Criminal Code Act applicable in southern states with the exception of Lagos stipulates that an individual is excluded from criminal liability if he or she is in 'such a state of mental disease... as to deprive him the capacity to understand what he is doing or of capacity to control his actions or of capacity to know not that he did the act'. However, those who are deluded can be criminally responsible as long as their delusions are not related to the crime for which they are convicted. There are no laws prohibiting the execution of prisoners who are mentally ill at the time the sentence is to be carried out. Intellectually disabled: An individual is excluded from criminal liability if he or she is in such a state of natural mental infamity.

The use of the death penalty in Nigeria has generated various opinions among people in society, with international communities clamoring for an end to the act, which according to them violates fundamental human rights. In 2017, the Nigerian government rejected the call by Amnesty International to halt the planned execution of some inmates on death row in Lagos State, and pointed out that the death penalty was expressly authorized by section 33 of the constitution of Nigeria. While more than 2,600 people were convicted and executed between 1970 and 1999, the rate of executions dropped dramatically after the fall of military government in May, 1999.

Europe

Belarus and the Death Penalty

This is the only UN member state in Europe that continues to carry out the death penalty, as they resumed executions after there had been none there the year before. 2015 and 2009 were the only two years in recorded history when Europe was completely free of executions.

Capital punishment has been a part of the country since gaining independence from the Soviet Union. The current national constitution prescribes this punishment for "grave crimes" while a few non-violent crimes can also be punishable by death.

The Criminal Code of the Republic of Belarus imposes capital punishment for the following acts: launching or conducting aggressive war, murder of a representative of a foreign state or international organization in order to provoke international complications or war, international terrorism, genocide, crimes against humanity, application of weapons of mass destruction under international treaties of the Republic of Belarus, violation of the war laws and usage, murder committed under aggravating circumstances, terrorism, treason connected with murder, conspiracy to seize state power, terrorist acts, sabotage, and murder of a police officer.

Over the years, the number of offences eligible for the death penalty and the type of convicts eligible for it have been reduced. In 1993, four economic crimes that would have resulted in death sentences during the Soviet era were removed from the list of capital offenses by a vote of Parliament and were replaced by prison terms without parole. This reduction was assisted by the introduction of life imprisonment in December 1997.

Since March 1, 1994, women are ineligible for capital punishment and persons under the age of 18 at the time of the crime or over 65 at the time of sentencing have been exempt from capital punishment since

January 2001. Also, those who are mentally ill may have their death sentence commuted and the president "may grant pardons to convicted citizens". From June 30, 2003 to June 30, 2005, President Alexander Lukashenko granted two pardons to death row inmates and denied one such request.

The method used to carry out the sentence is execution by shooting. The executioner is a member of the "committee for the execution of sentences," which also chooses the area where the execution will take place. On the day of execution, the convict is transported to a secret location where he is told by officials that all appeals have been rejected and then shot in the back of the head with a pistol. The whole process doesn't last more than ten minutes.

The following is a rough estimate of the number of executions carried out since 1990, as per the Belarusian Ministry of Internal Affairs (MVD):

1985 – 21	1986 – 10	1987 – 12	1988 – 12
1989 – 5	1990 – 20	1991 – 14	1992 – 24
1993 – 20	1994 – 24	1995 – 46	1997 – 46
1998 – 47	1999 – 13	2000 – 4	2001 – 7
2007 – 1	2008 – 4	2009 – 0	2010 – 2
2011 – 2	2012 – 1	2013 – 3	2014 – 3
2015 – 0	2016 – 4	2017 – 1	

Some of the recent executions include three of the four men on death row in the Belarusian capital Minsk who had been executed in a "shameful" death row "purge" as revealed by Amnesty International. The three men, Siarhei Khmialeuski, Ivan Kulesh and possibly Hyanadz Yakavitski, were executed with a gunshot to the back of the head while the fate of the fourth man on death row - Siarhei Vostrykau, sentenced to death on 19 May - is currently unknown. On the 17th of March, 2017, the country also sentenced 32-year-old Aliaksei Mikhalenya to death by the Gomel Regional Court of Belarus for two murders committed with particular cruelty, making it the first in 2017. This has however sparked new outcries from international communities on the urgent need for the country to make Europe a death penalty-free zone.

International organisations, such as the United Nations, have criticised the methods Belarus uses when carrying out capital punishment, and their insistence on maintaining it is one factor keeping the country out of the Council of Europe. There have also been accusations that the country doesn't inform families of the convicts before the eventual execution, as seen in the case of Siarhei Khmialeuski whose relatives arrived at the SIZO No1 prison in Minsk to visit him on death row, only to be informed he'd been executed on an unknown date in recent weeks.

Central and South America

The United States of America and the Death Penalty

Capital punishment is a legal penalty in the United States that is currently used by 31 states and the federal government. Its existence can be traced to the beginning of the American colonies. Historically, it is believed that Britain influenced America's use of the death penalty more than any other country.

When European settlers came to the new world, they brought the practice of capital punishment. The first recorded execution in the new colonies was that of Captain George Kendall in the Jamestown colony of Virginia in 1608. Kendall was executed for being a spy for Spain. In 1612, Virginia Governor Sir Thomas Dale enacted the Divine, Moral and Martial Laws, which provided the death penalty for even minor offenses such as stealing grapes, killing chickens, and trading with Indians.

The United States is the only Western country currently applying the death penalty, one of 57 countries worldwide applying it, and was the first to develop lethal injection as a method of execution, which has since been adopted by five other countries.

The major methods of execution in the United States are: electrocution, firing squad, hanging, use of the gas chambers and more recently, the use of lethal injection. From 1930 to 2002, there were 4,661 executions in the U.S., about two-thirds of them in the first 20 years.[15] Additionally, the United States Army executed 135 soldiers between 1916 and 1955 (the most recent).

The U.S. has thirty-two states using the death penalty as punishment for any of the Federal Government's forty-one capital offences, with over 1,392 executions since 1976. Eight states have abolished the death penalty since 2007 and no states have added. It should also be known that not all individuals awaiting execution are killed; some are released after their innocence has been proven, as seen in the statistics.

Regarded as one of the leading countries in the use of capital punishment for offences deemed 'grave', the United States seem to be keen on continuing the use of this form of punishment, tagged 'inhumane' by groups and people clamoring for its abolition.

Death Penalty In The Early And Mid-Twentieth Century

History has it that the abolitionist movement finds its roots in the writings of European theorists Montesquieu, Voltaire and Bentham, and English Quakers John Bellers and John Howard. However, it was Cesare Beccaria's 1767 essay, *On Crimes and Punishment*, that had an especially strong impact throughout the world. In the essay, Beccaria theorized that there was no justification for the State's taking of a life. The essay gave abolitionists an authoritative voice and renewed energy, one result of which was the abolition of the death penalty in Austria and Tuscany.

American intellectuals as well were influenced by Beccaria. The first attempted reforms of the death penalty in the U.S. occurred when Thomas Jefferson introduced a bill to revise Virginia's death penalty laws. The bill proposed that capital punishment be used only for the crimes of murder and treason. It was defeated by only one vote.

Also influential was Dr. Benjamin Rush, a signer of the Declaration of Independence and founder of the Pennsylvania Prison Society. Rush challenged the belief that the death penalty serves as a deterrent. In fact, Rush was an early believer in the "brutalization effect." He held that having a death penalty actually increased criminal conduct. Rush gained the support of Benjamin Franklin and Philadelphia attorney General William Bradford. Bradford, who would later become the U.S. Attorney General, led Pennsylvania to become the first state to consider degrees of murder based on culpability. In 1794, Pennsylvania repealed the death penalty for all offenses except first degree murder (Bohm, 1999; Randa, 1997; and Schabas, 1997).

The Bill of Rights adopted in 1789 included the Eighth Amendment which prohibited cruel and unusual punishment. The Fifth Amendment was drafted with language implying a possible use of the death penalty, requiring a grand jury indictment for "capital crime" and a due process of law for deprivation of "life" by the government. The Fourteenth Amendment adopted in 1868 also requires a due process of law for deprivation of life by any state.

Although some states abolished the death penalty in the mid-nineteenth century, it was actually the first half of the twentieth century that marked the beginning of the "Progressive Period" of reform in the United States. From 1907 to 1917, six states completely outlawed the death penalty and three limited it to the rarely committed crimes of treason and first-degree murder of a law enforcement official. However, this reform was short-lived. There was a frenzied atmosphere in the U.S., as citizens began to panic about the threat of revolution in the wake of the Russian Revolution. In addition, the U.S. had just entered World War I and there were intense class conflicts as socialists mounted the first serious challenge to capitalism. As a result, five of the six abolitionist states reinstated their death penalty by 1920 (Bedau, 1997 and Bohm, 1999).

In 1924, the use of cyanide gas was introduced, as Nevada sought a more humane way of executing its inmates. Gee Jon was a Chinese national and a member of the Hip Sing Tong criminal society from San Francisco, California. Gee was sentenced to death for the murder of an elderly member from another gang in Nevada and was the first person executed by lethal gas. The state tried to pump cyanide gas into Jon's cell while he slept, but this proved impossible, and the gas chamber was constructed (Bohm, 1999).

From the 1920s to the 1940s, there was a resurgence in the use of the death penalty. This was due, in part, to the writings of criminologists, who argued that the death penalty was a necessary social measure. In the United States, Americans were suffering through Prohibition and the Great Depression. There were more executions in the 1930s than in any other decade in American history, an average of 167 per year (Bohm, 1999 and Schabas, 1997).

In the 1950s, public sentiment began to turn away from capital punishment. Many allied nations either abolished or limited the death penalty, and in the U.S., the number of executions dropped dramatically. Whereas there were 1,289 executions in the 1940s, there were 715 in the 1950s, and the number fell even further to only 191 from 1960 to 1976. In 1966, support for capital punishment reached an all-time low. A Gallup poll showed support for the death penalty at only 42% (Bohm, 1999 and BJS, 1997).

In *Furman v. Georgia*, the U.S. Supreme Court considered a group of consolidated cases. The lead case involved an individual convicted under Georgia's death penalty statute, which featured a "unitary trial" procedure in which the jury was asked to return a verdict of guilt or innocence and, simultaneously, determine whether the defendant would be punished by death or life imprisonment. The last pre-*Furman* execution was that of convicted mass murder Luis Monge on June 2, 1967. In a 5-4 decision, the Supreme Court struck down the impositions of the death penalty in each of the consolidated cases as unconstitutional in violation of the Eighth and Fourteenth Amendments of the United States Constitution. The Supreme Court has never ruled the death penalty to be unconstitutional *per se*.

The *Furman* decision caused all death sentences pending at the time to be reduced to life imprisonment, and was described by scholars as a "legal bombshell". The next day, columnist Barry

Schweid, who U.S. Secretary of State John Kerry called "an Associated Press legend and the long-time dean of the State Department press corps", wrote that it was "unlikely" that the death penalty could exist anymore in the United States.

Nevertheless, capital punishment continued to be used by a majority of states and the federal government for various crimes, especially murder and rape, from the creation of the United States up to the beginning of the 1960s. Until then, "save for a few mavericks, no one gave any credence to the possibility of ending the death penalty by judicial interpretation of constitutional law", according to abolitionist Hugo Bedau.

THE DEATH PENALTY REINSTATED

Instead of abandoning capital punishment, 37 states enacted new death penalty statutes that attempted to address the concerns of White and Stewart in *Furman*. Some states responded by enacting mandatory death penalty statutes which prescribed a sentence of death for anyone convicted of certain forms of murder. White had hinted that such a scheme would meet his constitutional concerns in his *Furman* opinion. Other states adopted "bifurcated" trial and sentencing procedures, with various procedural limitations on the jury's ability to pronounce a death sentence designed to limit juror discretion.

Executions resumed on January 17, 1977, when Gary Gilmore gained international notoriety for demanding the implementation of his death sentence for two murders he committed and went before a firing squad in Utah. Although hundreds of individuals were sentenced to death in the United States during the

1970s and early 1980s, only ten people besides Gilmore (who had waived all of his appeal rights) were actually executed prior to 1984.

U.S NARROWS DOWN ON CASES ATTRACTING THE DEATH PENALTY

In 1977, the Supreme Court's *Coker v. Georgia* decision barred the death penalty for rape of an adult woman. Previously, the death penalty for rape of an adult had been gradually phased out in the United States, and at the time of the decision, Georgia and the U.S. Federal government were the only two jurisdictions to still retain the death penalty for that offense.

In the 1980 case *Godfrey v. Georgia*, the U.S. Supreme Court ruled that murder can be punished by death only if it involves a narrow and precise aggravating factor.

The U.S. Supreme Court has placed two major restrictions on the use of the death penalty. First, the case of *Atkins v. Virginia*, decided on June 20, 2002, held that the execution of intellectually disabled inmates is unconstitutional. Second, in 2005, the court's decision in *Roper v. Simmons* struck down executions for offenders under the age of 18 at the time of the crime.

In the 2008 case *Kennedy v. Louisiana*, the court also held 5-4 that the death penalty is unconstitutional when applied to non-homicidal crimes against the person, including child rape. Only two death row inmates (both in Louisiana) were affected by the decision. Nevertheless, the ruling came less than five months before the 2008 presidential election and was criticized by both major party candidates Barack Obama and John McCain .

As of October 1, 2014, men accounted for 98% of people on death row and 99% of executions since 1976.

THE U.S AND DEATH PENALTY STATISTICS

Within the context of the overall murder rate, the death penalty cannot be said to be widely or routinely used in the United States in recent years. The average has been about one death sentence for every 200 murder convictions.

Alabama has the highest *per capita* rate of death sentences. This is because Alabama was one of the few states that allowed judges to override a jury recommendation in favor of life imprisonment, a possibility it removed in March 2017.

The distribution of death sentences among states is loosely proportional to their populations and murder rates. California, which is the most populous state, has also the largest death row with over 700 inmates. Wyoming, which is the least populous state, has only one condemned man.

But executions are more frequent (and happen more quickly after sentencing) in conservative states. Texas, which is the second most populous state of the Union, carried out over 500 executions during the post-*Furman* era, more than a third of the national total. California has carried out only 13 executions during the same period.

Below are the death penalty statistics in 2016 by Statistic Brain which listed its sources of information as NAACP Legal Defense Fund's *Death Row, USA* Gallup poll and Bureau of Justice Statistics:

Death Penalty Statistics

Number of U.S States with the death penalty- 32

Total number of executions since 1976- 1,392

Current number of death row inmates- 3,035

Percent of people who support the death penalty- 65%

Percent of counties in the U.S. that have not had one person executed in 45 years- 85%

Number of people released from death row with evidence of their innocence- 130

Number of clemencies that have been granted- 268

Death sentences given in 2014- 72

Year over the past decade with the most death sentences given- The year 2000 with 223

Average cost of a death penalty case- $2.4 million

Number of states where the governor has the sole authority to grant clemency- 16.

In the statistics above, one would see that in spite of the expensive cost of a death penalty case, the country has insisted on the practice, showing a resolve to either completely end crimes or just as a way of showing strict judicial powers. It is also worthy of note that the percentage of people who still support the use of the death penalty is 65%, which is more than the average percentage of the population and shows that there is a firm belief in its effectiveness, even if there are disparities on the methods to be used.

The United States, being a multi-ethnic society, has often times been tagged racist in their conduct and most especially in the discharge of judicial duties. The country has been accused of leniency in cases of their citizens and highhandedness in the case of the immigrants living in the country. Will it then be right to conclude that the rate of other races will be higher than that of Caucasians in the application of the death penalty? Or even that Caucasians are less susceptible to committing capital offences than other races, e.g. African Americans? The statistics below are expected to answer these questions.

African Americans made up 41% of death row inmates while making up only 12.6% of the general population. They have made up 34% of those actually executed since 1976. However, this is an under-representation relative to the proportion of convicted murderers: 52.5% of all homicide offenders between 1980 and 2008 were African Americans. According to a 2003 Amnesty International report, African Americans and Caucasians were the victims of murder in almost equal numbers, yet 80% of the people executed since 1977 were convicted of murders involving Caucasian victims.

Approximately 13.5% of death row inmates are of Hispanic or Latino descent, while they make up 17.4% of the general population.

Race of Defendants Executed

Caucasian- 56%

African American- 35%

Hispanic- 8%

Other races- 2%

Race of Victim in Death Penalty Case

Caucasian- 76%

African American- 15%

Hispanic- 6%

Other races- 3%

Total number of death row exonerations- 138

Total number of people currently on death row- 3,261.

Next, we will look at the statistics on the number of people executed with each method of execution used in the country:

Executions by Method Statistics

Firing Squad- 3

Hanging- 3

Gas Chamber-11

Electrocution- 158

Lethal Injection- 1220.

The statistics above show that there is a movement away from more painful methods of execution and towards a more 'humane' form, which is the use of drug combinations in lethal injections. However, a study of executions carried out in the U.S. between 1977 and 2001 indicated that at least 34 of the 749 executions, or 4.5%, involved" unanticipated problems or delays that caused, at least arguably, unnecessary agony for the prisoner or that reflect gross incompetence of the executioner", but the U.S. Supreme Court has insisted that lethal injection does not constitute cruel and unusual punishment. The debate on whether the use of lethal injection as a method of executing prisoners will be extensively discussed in the course of this book.

Executions by Region

South- 1,142

Texas and Oklahoma- 634

Midwest- 172

West- 85

Northeast- 4

Number of Executions by Year

2015- *9 (Through March)*		2014- *35*	2013-*39*
2012- *43*	2011- *43*	2010- *38*	2009-*52*
2008- *37*	2007- *42*	2006- *53*	2005- *60*
2004- *59*	2003- *65*	2002- *71*	2001- *66*
2000- *85*	1999- *98*	1998- *68*	1997- *74*
1996- *45*	1995- *56*	1994- *31*	1993- *38*
1992- *31*	1990- *23*	1989- *16*	1988- *11*
1987- *25*	1986- *18*	1985- *18*	1984- *21*
1983- *5*	1982- *2*	1981- *1*	1980- *0*
1979- *2*	1978- *0*	1977- *0.*	

It seems as if Americans are beginning to have a change of heart as to the effectiveness of the death penalty. There are even reports that there are new alternatives being suggested to replace capital punishment. The disclosure in a 2015 Gallup poll indicates support for the death penalty in the U.S. is at a 40-year low, with a 63% percent favorability rating a stark contrast to the 80% in the 1990s.

A recent edition of the NAACP's statistics also shows a continuation of the downward trend in the overall death row population, though California (with 731 inmates) - the state with the largest death row - recorded an increase. The next leading states were Florida (412), Texas (298), Pennsylvania (198), and Alabama (197), all of which registered decreases on death row. The total population of 3108 inmates as of April 1st, 2013, represents a 12% decline from the same date 10 years ago, when there were 3,525 inmates on death row.

Since the last report was released in January, death row populations in 11 states and the Federal system have decreased. The report also contains racial breakdown of death rows, executions and victims in cases that resulted in executions. The states with the highest percentage of minorities on death row were Delaware (78%) and Texas (71%), among those with at least 10 inmates on death row.

The Bureau of Justice statistics also recently received its annual review of the death penalty in the U.S, focusing on 2011. The report noted the continued decline in the use of the death penalty in recent years. In 2011, 80 new inmates were received under sentence of death, the lowest number since 1973, a 27% decrease from the year before. Executions also declined to 43 compared with 46 in 2010. The average time between sentencing and execution in 2011 was 16.5 years, 20 months longer than for those executed in 2010. The number of people on death row in the U.S. dropped to 3,082, marking the eleventh consecutive year in which the size of death row decreased.

METHODS OF EXECUTION IN THE U.S.

HANGING

Hanging is the oldest method of execution in the United States as it was the primary method of execution used until the 1890s. This method fell into disfavor in the 20th century after many botched attempts, and was replaced by electrocution as the most common method. There have been only three executions by hanging since 1977: Westley Dodd (WA 1993), Charles Campbell (WA 1994), and Billy Bailey (DE 1996).

Currently, only three states, Delaware, New Hampshire, and Washington, authorize hanging as a method of execution, all as an alternative to lethal injection, depending upon the choice of the inmate, whether injection is "impractical" or the possibility of lethal injection being held unconstitutional. Since the reinstatement of the death penalty in 1976, only 3 out of 1,389 (0.3%) convicted murderers executed were by hanging. Most recently, Billy Bailey chose hanging in Delaware on January 25, 1996, telling a visitor, "I'm not going to let them put me to sleep."

For execution by this method, the inmate may be weighed the day before the execution, and a rehearsal is done using a sandbag of the same weight as the prisoner. This is to determine the length of 'drop' necessary to ensure a quick death. If the rope is too long, the inmate could be decapitated, and if it is too short, the strangulation could take as long as 45 minutes. The rope, which should be 3/4-inch to 1 1/4-inches in diameter, must be boiled and stretched to eliminate spring or coiling. The knot should be lubricated with wax or soap "to ensure a smooth sliding action," according to the 1969 U.S. Army manual (The Corrections Professional, 1996 and Hillman, 1992).

Immediately before the execution, the prisoner's hands and legs are secured, he or she is blindfolded, and the noose is placed around the neck, with the knot behind the left ear. The execution takes place when a trap-door is opened and the prisoner falls through. The prisoner's weight should cause a rapid fracture-dislocation of the neck. However, instantaneous death rarely occurs (Weisberg, 1991). However, if the inmate has strong neck muscles, is very light, if the 'drop' is too short, or the noose has been wrongly positioned, the fracture-dislocation is not rapid and death results from slow asphyxiation. If this occurs, the face becomes engorged, the tongue protrudes, the eyes pop, the body defecates, and violent movements of the limbs occur (The Corrections Professional, 1996 and Weisberg, 1991).

Another procedure that is done prior to execution using this method is to review the condemned offender's file to determine if there are any unusual characteristics the offender possesses that might warrant deviation from field instructions on hanging. A physical examination and measuring process is conducted to assure almost instant death and a minimum of bruising. If careful measuring and planning is not done, strangulation, obstructed blood flow, or beheading could result. At the appropriate time on execution day, the inmate, in restraints, is escorted to the gallows area and is placed standing over a hinged trap door from which the offender will be dropped.

Following the offender's last statement, a hood is placed over the offender's head. Restraints are also applied. If the offender refuses to stand or cannot stand, he is placed on a collapse board. A determination of the proper amount of the drop through the trap door is calculated using a standard military execution chart for hanging. It must be based on the prisoner's weight, to deliver 1260 foot pounds of force to the neck. The noose is then placed snugly around the convict's neck, which will cause the neck to snap. The trap door then opens, and the convict drops. A button mechanically releases the trap door and escorts then move to the lower floor location to assist in the removal of the offender's body.

ELECTROCUTION

The first electric chair was built in 1890 as a more humane alternative method of execution than hanging. The first person executed using this method was William Kemmler in 1890 and the last state to adopt electrocution as a method of execution was in 1949. It gained prominence as the most common method of execution in the United States.

Presently, no state uses electrocution as the sole method of execution, but nine states provide for electrocution as an alternative method to lethal injection, depending upon the choice of the inmate, the date of execution or sentence, or the possibility of the method being held unconstitutional. Since its reinstatement in 1976, 158 convicted murderers executed were by electric chair: Florida 44, Virginia 31, Alabama 24, Georgia 23, Louisiana 20, South Carolina 7, Indiana 3, Nebraska 3, Kentucky 1, Arkansas 1, and Tennessee 1. The last execution by electric chair was January 16, 2013 in the case of Robert Charles Gleason Jr. in Virginia.

For execution by the electric chair, the person is usually shaved and strapped to a chair with belts that cross their chest, groin, legs, and arms. A metal skullcap-shaped electrode is attached to the scalp and forehead over a sponge moistened with saline. The sponge must not be too wet or the saline short-circuits the electric current, and not too dry as it would then have a very high resistance.

An additional electrode is moistened with conductive jelly (Electro-Crème) and attached to a portion of the prisoner's leg that has been shaved to reduce resistance to electricity. The prisoner is then blindfolded (Hillman, 1992 and Weisberg, 1991). After the execution team has withdrawn to the observation room, the warden signals the executioner, who pulls a handle to connect the power supply. A jolt of between 500 and 2000 volts, which lasts for about 30 seconds, is given.

The current surges and is then turned off, at which time the body is seen to relax. The doctors wait a few seconds for the body to cool down and then check to see if the inmate's heart is still beating. If it is, another jolt is applied. This process continues until the prisoner is dead. The prisoner's hands often grip the chair and there may be violent movement of the limbs which can result in dislocation or fractures. The tissues swell. Defecation occurs. Steam or smoke rises and there is a smell of burning.

FIRING SQUAD

Only two states currently use the firing squad as a method of execution: Utah and Oklahoma, all as an alternative to lethal injection. On March 23, 2015, firing squad was reauthorized in Utah as a viable method of execution if and only if the state is unable to obtain the drugs necessary to carry out a lethal injection execution. Prior to this reauthorization, firing squad was only a method of execution in Utah if chosen by an inmate before lethal injection became the sole means of execution.

The Utah statute authorizing execution by firing squad only provides: "If the judgment of death is to be carried out by shooting, the executive director of the department or his designee shall select a five-person firing squad of peace officers."

Shooting can be carried out by a single executioner who fires from short range at the back of the head (or neck as in China). The traditional firing squad is made up of three to six shooters per prisoner who stand or kneel opposite the condemned, who is usually tied to a chair or to a stake. Normally the shooters aim at the chest, since this is easier to hit than the head, causing rupture of the heart, great vessels, and lungs so that the condemned person dies of hemorrhage and shock. It is not unusual for the officer in charge to have to give the prisoner a pistol shot to the head to finish them off after the initial volley has failed to kill them.

At the appropriate time, the condemned offender is led to the execution area or chamber, which is used for both lethal injection and firing squad executions. The offender is placed in a specially designed chair which has a pan beneath it to catch and conceal blood and other fluids. Restraints are applied to the offender's arms, legs, chest and head. A head restraint is applied loosely around the offender's neck to hold their neck and head in an upright position.

The offender is dressed in a dark blue outfit with a white cloth circle attached by Velcro to the area over the offender's heart. Behind the offender are sandbags to absorb the volley and prevent ricochets. Approximately 20 feet directly in front of the offender is a wall. This wall has firing ports for each member of the firing squad. The weapons used are 30_30 calibre rifles. No special ammunition is used. Following the offender's statement, a hood is placed over the offender's head. The warden leaves the room.

The firing squad members stand in the firing position. They support their rifles on the platform rests. With their rifle barrels in the firing ports, the team members aim through open sights at the white cloth circle on the offender's chest. On the command to fire, the squad fires simultaneously. One squad member has a blank charge in their weapon but no member knows which member is designated to receive this blank charge.

In recent history only three inmates have been executed by firing squad, all in Utah: Gary Gilmore (1977), John Albert Taylor, and Ronnie Lee Gardner (2010). While the method was popular with the military in times of war, there has been only one such execution since the Civil War: Private Eddie Slovak in WWII.

LETHAL GAS

The use of a gas chamber for execution was inspired by the use of poisonous gas in World War I, as well as the popularity of the gas oven as a means of suicide. Nevada became the first state to adopt execution by lethal gas in 1924 and carried out the first execution in 1924. Since then it has served as the means of carrying out the death sentence thirty-one times. Lethal gas was seen as an improvement over other forms of execution, because it was less violent and did not disfigure or mutilate the body. The last execution by lethal gas took place in Arizona in 1999.

Only four states, Arizona, California, Missouri, and Wyoming, currently authorize lethal gas as a method of execution, all as an alternative to lethal injection, depending upon the choice of the inmate, the date of the execution or sentence, or the possibility of lethal injection being held unconstitutional. Since the reinstatement of the death penalty in 1976, 11 out of 1,389 (01.0%) convicted murderers executed were by the administration of lethal gas. Most recently, Walter LeGrand elected lethal gas in Arizona on March 3, 1999.

For execution by this method, the condemned person is strapped to a chair in an airtight chamber. Below the chair rests a pail of sulfuric acid. A long stethoscope is typically affixed to the inmate so that a doctor outside the chamber can pronounce death. Once everyone has left the chamber, the room is sealed. The warden then gives a signal to the executioner who flicks a lever that releases crystals of sodium cyanide into the pail. This causes a chemical reaction that releases hydrogen cyanide gas (Weisberg, 1991).

The prisoner is instructed to breathe deeply to speed up the process. Most prisoners, however, try to hold their breath, and some struggle. The inmate does not lose consciousness immediately and they usually go into wild convulsions. A heart monitor attached to the inmate is read in the control room, and after the warden pronounces the inmate dead, ammonia is pumped into the execution chamber to neutralize the gas. Exhaust fans then remove the inert fumes from the chamber into two scrubbers that contain water and serve as a neutralizing agent. The neutralizing process takes approximately 30 minutes from the time the offender's death is determined. Death is estimated to usually occur within 6 to 18 minutes of the lethal gas emissions.

As of April 17, 2015, Oklahoma introduced death by nitrogen gas as an alternative to lethal injection if the necessary drugs cannot be found or if that method is found unconstitutional. Nitrogen is a naturally occurring gas in the atmosphere, and death would be caused by forcing the inmate to breathe only nitrogen, thereby depriving him or her of oxygen.

LETHAL INJECTION

This is the practice of injecting one or more drugs into a person (typically a barbiturate, paralytic, and potassium solution) for the express purpose of causing immediate death. The main application of this procedure is capital punishment, but the term may also be applied in a broader sense to include euthanasia and suicide. It first renders the person unconscious, and then stops the breathing and heart, in that order.

Lethal injection was first proposed on January 17, 1888, by Julius Mount Bleyer, a New York doctor who praised it as being cheaper than hanging. Bleyer's idea was never used due to a series of botched executions and the eventual rise of public disapproval of electrocutions. Nazi Germany developed the Action T4 euthanasia program as one of its methods of disposing of *Lebensunwertes Leben* ("life unworthy of life").The British Royal Commission on Capital Punishment (1949–53) also considered lethal injection, but eventually ruled it out after pressure from the British Medical Association (BMA).

Lethal injection gained popularity in the late 20th century as a form of execution intended to supplant other methods, notably electrocution, gas inhalation, hanging and firing squad, that were considered to be less humane. It is now the most common form of execution in the United States. In 1977, Oklahoma became the first state to adopt lethal injection. Texas performed the first execution by lethal injection in 1982 with the execution of Charlie Brooks.

Presently, 20 states authorize lethal injection as the sole method of execution. Sixteen other states provide for lethal injection as the primary method of execution, but provide alternative methods depending upon the choice of the inmate, the date of the execution or sentence, or the possibility of the method being held unconstitutional. Since 2008, almost 90% of all U.S. executions have been by lethal injection.

Lethal injection procedure in U.S. executions

The condemned person is strapped onto a gurney; two intravenous cannulae ("IVs") are inserted, one in each arm. Only one is necessary to carry out the execution; the other is reserved as a backup in the event the primary line fails. A line leading from the IV line in an adjacent room is attached to the prisoner's IV and secured, so that the line does not snap during the injections.

The arm of the condemned person is swabbed with alcohol before the cannula is inserted. The needles and equipment used are sterilized. Questions have been raised about why these precautions against infection are performed despite the purpose of the injection being death. The several explanations include: cannulae are sterilized during manufacture, so using sterile ones is routine medical procedure. Secondly, the prisoner could receive a stay of execution after the cannulae have been inserted, as happened in the case of James Autry in October 1983 (he was eventually executed on March 14, 1984). Third, the use of unsterilized equipment would be a hazard to prison personnel.

Following the connection of the lines, saline drips are started in both arms. This, too, is standard medical procedure: it must be ascertained that the IV lines are not blocked, ensuring the chemicals have not precipitated in the IV lines and blocked the needle, preventing the drugs from reaching the subject. A heart monitor is attached so prison officials can determine when death has occurred

Typically, three drugs are used in lethal injection: Sodium thiopental is used to induce unconsciousness, pancuronium bromide (Pavulon) to cause muscle paralysis and respiratory arrest, and potassium chloride to stop the heart. In most states, the execution of the condemned involves three separate injections (in sequential order).

However, states have developed new lethal protocols used in their executions as seen in the case of the Ohio protocol, developed after the incomplete execution of Romell Broom. This new protocol ensures the rapid and painless onset of anaesthesia by only using sodium thiopental and eliminating the use of Pavulon and potassium as the second and third drugs, respectively. It also provides for a secondary fail-safe measure using an intramuscular injection of midazolam and hydromorphone in the event that intravenous administration of the sodium thiopental proves problematic. The first state to switch to using midazolam as the first drug in a new three-drug protocol was Florida on October 15, 2013. Then on November 14, 2013, Ohio made the same move.

In the brief for the U.S. courts written by accessories, the state of Ohio implies that they were unable to find any physicians willing to participate in developing protocols for executions by lethal injection, as this would be a violation of medical ethics such as the Geneva Promise. Such physicians would be thrown out of the medical community and shunned for engaging in such deeds, even if they could not lawfully be stripped of their license.

On December 8, 2009, Kenneth Biros became the first person executed using Ohio's new single-drug execution protocol. He was pronounced dead at 11:47 am EST, 10 minutes after receiving the injection. On September 10, 2010, Washington became the second state to use the single-drug Ohio protocol with the execution of Cal Coburn Brown, who was proclaimed dead within two minutes after receiving the single-drug injection of sodium thiopental. Currently, eight states (Arizona, Georgia, Idaho, Missouri, Ohio, South Dakota, Texas, and Washington) have used the single-drug execution protocol. Five additional states (Arkansas, Kentucky, Louisiana, North Carolina, and Tennessee) have announced that they are switching to a single-drug protocol, but as of April 2014 have not executed anyone since switching protocols.

Ethics of lethal injection

The American Medical Association (AMA) believes that a physician's opinion on capital punishment is a personal decision. Since the AMA is founded on preserving life, they argue that a doctor "should not be a participant" in executions in any professional capacity with the exception of "certifying death, provided that the condemned has been declared dead by another person" and "relieving the acute suffering of a condemned person while awaiting execution". Amnesty International argues that the AMA's position effectively "prohibits doctors from participating in executions." The AMA, however, does not have the authority to prohibit doctors from participation in lethal injection, nor does it have the authority to revoke medical licenses, since this is the responsibility of the individual states.

Typically, most states do not require that physicians administer the drugs for lethal injection, but many states do require that physicians be present to pronounce or certify death.

DIFFERENT PERSPECTIVES ON THE USE OF CAPITAL PUNISHMENT

This chapter will dwell on the views of different people, sects, religions and moral outlooks on the justification for or against the use of the death penalty for capital offences in the world. These views have been classified into the following sub-headings for the easy understanding of the work of study:

Religious Views

Traditional Views

Moralistic Views

Religious Views

The question of whether to apply capital punishment for especially severe or heinous crimes is a moral dilemma for civilized societies across the world. In view of this, this section will discuss the different opinions of major religions practiced in the world on the issue of the death penalty both in support and against. It will however be streamlined to the following religions believed to be the most commonly practiced:

Christianity

Islam

Buddhism

Christianity and the Death Penalty

As explained earlier, the topic of capital punishment is a continuing source of national discussion and debate and Christianity is not an exception.

Does Scripture mandate, prohibit, or permit capital punishment? Christians are divided on this issue as they argue both for and against the death penalty using secular arguments, but like other religious, people they often make an additional case based on the tenets of their faith. For much of history, the Christian churches accepted that capital punishment was a necessary part of the mechanisms of society.

Pope Innocent III (1161 –1216), for example, put forward the proposition: "The secular power can, without mortal sin, exercise judgment of blood, provided that it punishes with justice, not out of hatred, with prudence, not precipitation." The Roman Catechism, issued in 1566, stated that the power of life and death had been entrusted by God to the civil authorities. The use of this power did not embody the act of murder, but rather a supreme obedience to God's commandments.

In the high Middle Ages and later, the Holy See authorized that heretics be turned over to the secular authorities for execution and the laws of Vatican City from 1929 to 1969 included the death penalty for anyone who tried to assassinate the Pope.

Throughout the first half of the twentieth century the consensus amongst Catholic theologians remained in favour of capital punishment in those cases deemed suitably extreme.

However, by the end of this century opinions were changing. In 1980, the National Conference of Catholic Bishops published an almost entirely negative statement on capital punishment, approved by a majority vote of those present, though not by the required two-thirds majority of the entire conference.

In 1997 the Vatican announced changes to the Catechism, thus making it more in line with John Paul II's 1995 encyclical *The Gospel of Life*. The amendments include the following statement concerning capital punishment:

Assuming that the guilty party's identity and responsibility have been fully determined, the traditional teaching of the Church does not exclude recourse to the death penalty, if this is the only possible way of effectively defending human lives against the unjust aggressor.

If, however, non-lethal means are sufficient to defend and protect people's safety from the aggressor, authority will limit itself to such means, as these are more in keeping with the concrete conditions of the common good and more in conformity with the dignity of the human person.

Today, in fact, as a consequence of the possibilities which the state has for effectively preventing crime, by rendering one who has committed an offence incapable of doing harm--without definitively taking away from him the possibility of redeeming himself-- the cases in which the execution of the offender is an absolute necessity are rare, if not practically non-existent.

Pope John Paul II, The Gospel of Life

Points in favor of the death penalty

The principal argument of Christians who believe that capital punishment should not be abolished is that because life is sacred, those who wrongfully take another human life must lose their own lives too. This is a form of restitution; a matter of justice— the state purging itself of those who shed innocent blood. Proponents of this position cite three scriptural arguments:

Genesis 9:6 says, "Whoever sheds the blood of man, by man shall his blood be shed; for in the image of God has God made man." This is part of the larger covenant that God made with Noah after the flood. It not only reflects the great value of human life, but also gives the reason for that value: Man is made in God's image. The absolute language of Genesis 9:6 suggests that all those who kill another human being must be killed. And since this mandate was given long before the Mosaic Law to all who survived the flood, it apparently has universal application."

The Law, as given to Moses on Mt. Sinai, ordained execution for several offenses: murder (but not accidental killings), striking or cursing a parent, kidnapping, adultery, incest, bestiality, sodomy, rape of a betrothed virgin, witchcraft, incorrigible delinquency, breaking the Sabbath, blasphemy, sacrificing to false gods, oppressing the weak, and other transgressions (See Exod. 21, 22, 35; Lev. 20 & 24; Deut. 21-24).

While no New Testament passage expressly mandates capital punishment, several imply its appropriateness. For example, in Romans 13:1-7 Paul calls his readers to submit to the authority of civil government, reminding them that "if you do wrong, be afraid, for he [the authority] does not bear the sword for nothing." In its ultimate use, the word *sword* implies execution.

The death penalty is consistent with Old Testament Biblical teaching, and suggests that God created the death penalty and the Old Testament specifies 36 capital offences including crimes such as idolatry, magic and blasphemy, as well as murder. However, many Christians don't think that is a convincing argument; they say that there are 35 capital offences, in addition to murder, described in the Old Testament. As these are no longer capital offences, Christians say it is inconsistent to preserve murder alone as a capital crime.

The New Testament and the Death Penalty

The New Testament embodies what must be the most famous execution in history, that of Jesus on the cross. But paradoxically, although the tone of the whole of the New Testament is one of forgiveness, it seems to take the right of the state to execute offenders for granted.

In Matthew 7:2 we read "Whatever measure you deal out to others will be dealt back to you", though this is unspecific as to whether it is God who is doing the dealing, or the state.

In Matthew 15:4 Jesus says "He who speaks evil of father or mother, let him surely die".
Despite the fact that Jesus himself refrains from using violence, he at no point denies the state's authority to exact capital punishment.

At the moment that Pilate has to decide whether or not to crucify Jesus, Jesus tells him that the power to make this decision has been given to him by God (John 19:11).

Paul makes an apparent reference to the death penalty when he writes that the magistrate who holds authority "does not bear the sword in vain; for he is the servant of God to execute His wrath on the wrongdoer" (Romans 13:4).

Capital punishment affirms the commandment that 'thou shalt not kill' by affirming the seriousness of the crime of murder.

This argument is based on interpreting the commandment as meaning "thou shalt not murder", but some Christians argue that the 'Thou shalt not kill' commandment is an absolute prohibition on killing.

Another argument used by Christians who support the death penalty is the fact that the state acts not on its own authority but as the agent of God, who does have legal power over life and death. This argument is well expressed by St Augustine, who wrote:

The same divine law which forbids the killing of a human being allows certain exceptions, as when God authorises killing by a general law or when He gives an explicit commission to an individual for a limited time. Since the agent of authority is but a sword in the hand, and is not responsible for the killing, it is in no way contrary to the commandment, 'Thou shalt not kill' to wage war at God's bidding, or for the representatives of the State's authority to put criminals to death, according to law or the rule of rational justice.

Augustine, *The City of God*

They also argue that the criminal, by choosing to commit a particular crime, has also chosen to surrender his life to the state if caught. Even when there is question of the execution of a condemned man, the state does not dispose of the individual's right to life. In this case it is reserved for the public power to deprive the condemned person of the enjoyment of life in expiation of his crime when, by his crime, he has already dispossessed himself of his right to life.

Pope Pius XII

Arguments against the death penalty

Israel was a theocracy, a nation ruled directly by God. Therefore, its Law was unique. Executing false teachers and those who sacrificed to false gods are examples of provisions that sprang from Israel's unique position as a nation of God called to be holy. When Israel ceased to exist as a nation, its Law was nullified. Even the execution of murderers stemmed, in part, from God's special relationship to Israel. Numbers 35:33 says that the blood of a murder victim "pollutes the land," a pollution that must be cleansed by the death of the murderer. If the murderer could not be found, an animal was to be sacrificed to God to purge the community of guilt (Deut. 21).

Christ's death on the cross ended the requirement for blood recompense and blood sacrifice. The sacrifice of Jesus, the Lamb of God, replaced the sacrifice of animals. His death also made it unnecessary to execute murderers to maintain human dignity and value because the crucifixion forever established human value. Hebrews 9:14 says, "How much more, then, will the blood of Christ, who through the eternal Spirit offered himself unblemished to God, cleanse our consciences from acts that lead to death, so that we may serve the living God!"

Christ's teaching emphasizes forgiveness and willingness to suffer evil rather than resist it by force. This may not be definitive on the issue of the state's authority to execute, but it does demonstrate a different approach to responding to evil than that established on Mt. Sinai. Christ's example in not demanding death for the adulteress supports this argument (John 8).

Only God should create and destroy life. This argument is used to oppose abortion and euthanasia as well, and many Christians believe that God commanded "Thou shalt not kill" (Exodus 21:13), and that this is a clear instruction with no exceptions. There are however arguments to counter this assertion.

The Bible's teachings are inconsistent, as it speaks in favour of the death penalty for murder. But it also prescribes it for 35 other crimes that we no longer regard as deserving the death penalty. In order to be consistent, humanity should remove the death penalty for murder. Secondly, modern society has alternative punishments available which were not used in Biblical times, and these make the death penalty unnecessary.

Christianity is based on forgiveness and compassion, and capital punishment is incompatible with a teaching that emphasises forgiveness and compassion.

Some Christians argue that in many countries the imposition of the death penalty is biased against the poor. Since Christian teachings support the poor, Christians should not support the death penalty.

Abolition is in line with support for life, and capital punishment is inconsistent with the general Christian stance that life should always be supported. This stance is most often taught in issues such as abortion and euthanasia, but consistency requires Christians to apply it across the board.

In spite of the above seemingly convincing arguments for and against the use of capital punishment in Christianity, there are other assertions that refute both sides and might be considered neutral. Some of these are:

Scripture includes many provisions for capital punishment. The Mosaic Law significantly limited the scope of Genesis 9:6. For example, individuals guilty of manslaughter or accidentally causing another's death were exempted from the death penalty.

Perhaps the most compelling arguments against capital punishment are the examples of capital criminals who were not executed, such as Cain, Moses, and David. And not only did Jesus refuse to condemn the woman caught in adultery, but He also suggested that only those without sin were qualified to perform the execution. Jewish interpretation of Old Testament Law reflected a great reluctance to impose the death penalty. For example, circumstantial evidence wasn't admitted. The two eyewitnesses (Num. 35) had to have warned the accused he was about to commit a capital crime. If the two witnesses' testimonies differed, the accused was acquitted. Men presumed to lack compassion could not rule on a capital case.

New Testament passages assume the existence of the death penalty but don't take a position one way or the other. Romans 13 comes closest to speaking of the state's authority to execute, but significantly it refers to the state's *authority*, not *obligation*, to execute.

This is consistent with the position that states are permitted, not mandated or prohibited, the use of this sanction.

Those who believe that Scripture mandates or permits capital punishment must move on to another question: What conditions does Scripture give before the state may exercise capital punishment? The Old Testament Law did not simply address the "whether" of capital punishment; it also spoke of the "how." These provisions need not be literally carried out today for our death-penalty statutes to meet biblical standards. For example, Deuteronomy 17 required the condemning witnesses to throw the first stones. This is impossible today, because stoning is not a current method of execution. However, the principle is that witnesses were held *responsible* for the consequences of their testimony, encouraging truthfulness. Here are some other principles drawn from the Mosaic Law's procedures:

PROPORTIONALITY: Exodus 21:23-25 establishes that punishment must be proportional to the offense. The extreme sanction of death should be considered only in the most serious offenses.

CERTAINTY OF GUILT: Before a murderer could be executed, two witnesses had to confirm his guilt (Deut. 17:6; Num. 35:30). This was a very high standard of proof. The Bible says nothing of circumstantial evidence.

INTENT: Numbers 35:22- 24 established that capital punishment could not be imposed when the offender did not act intentionally.

DUE PROCESS: Several provisions of the Law ensured that executions took place only after appropriate judicial procedures (see Num. 35; Deut. 17). The issue was not simply whether the accused was guilty, but whether he also had a fair chance to prove his innocence.

RELUCTANCE TO EXECUTE: Although the Law may sound bloodthirsty, it was applied with great restraint. In Ezekiel 33:11 God laments, "As sure as I live . . . I take no pleasure in the death of the wicked, but rather that they turn from their ways and live." The Lawgiver Himself was reluctant to impose the death penalty, preferring that the wrongdoers repent. Reluctance is *not* refusal. But it does imply that execution should be a last resort, and, as Ezekiel 33 suggests, repentance or contrition could commute the death sentence.

Islam and the Death Penalty

As controversial as the issue of capital punishment is, in Islam the law guides Muslims' views on this, clearly establishing the sanctity of human life and the prohibition against taking a human life but making a clear exception for punishment enacted under legal justice.

The Quran clearly establishes that killing is forbidden, but just as clearly establishes conditions under which capital punishment may be enacted:

If anyone kills a person—unless it is for murder or for spreading mischief in the land—it would be as if he killed all people. And if anyone saves a life, it would be as if he saved the life of all people. (Quran 5:32)

The death penalty has been outlawed in a majority of the world's nations, but continues to be used widely in the Middle East. One of the main reasons for the use of capital punishment in this region is that it is clearly permitted by the Quran, the Islamic holy text.

As such, most nations that consider Islam to be the state religion (including Iraq, Kuwait, Qatar and the United Arab Emirates, among others) and all Islamic states (including Afghanistan, Bahrain, Brunei, Iran, Mauritania, Oman, Pakistan, Saudi Arabia and Yemen) permit and often encourage the use of the death penalty.

Several verses in the Quran support the use of capital punishment when used as a lawful means of seeking justice. Life is sacred, according to Islam and most other world faiths. But how can one hold life sacred, yet still support capital punishment? The Quran answers:

Take not life, which God has made sacred, except by way of justice and law. Thus, does He command you, so that you may learn wisdom. (Q6:151)

Basically, this means that although murder is considered a sin, it is permissible to utilize capital punishment when required by law. The key point is that one may take life only "by way of justice and law." In Islam, therefore, the death penalty can be applied by a court as punishment for the most serious of crimes. Ultimately, one's eternal punishment is in God's hands, but there is a place for punishment enacted by society in this life as well. The spirit of the Islamic penal code is to save lives, promote justice, and prevent corruption and tyranny.

Muslims who support the death penalty believe that its use provides an effective deterrent against crime and as such, helps to promote justice. Islamic law permits the use of the death penalty as a punishment against *intentional murder* and *Fasaad fi al-ardh*, which translates to "spreading mischief throughout the land."

This type of crime is interpreted in a variety of ways, but can include rape, adultery, treason, apostasy, piracy, sodomy and homosexual behavior. Islamic philosophy holds that a harsh punishment serves as a deterrent to serious crimes that harm individual victims or those that threaten to destabilize the foundation of society.

Intentional Murder

The Quran legislates that the death penalty for murder is available, although forgiveness and compassion are strongly encouraged. In Islamic law, the murder victim's family is given a choice to either insist on the death penalty or to pardon the perpetrator and accept monetary compensation for their loss (Q2:178).

Fasaad Fi al- Ardh

Fasaad Fi al- Ardh, being the second crime for which capital punishment can be applied, is a bit more open to interpretation, and it is here that Islam has developed a reputation for harsher legal justice than what is practiced elsewhere in the world. "Spreading mischief in the land" can mean many different things, but it is generally interpreted to refer to those crimes that affect the community as a whole and destabilize society. Crimes that have fallen under this description include:

Treason/apostasy (when one leaves the faith and joins the enemy in fighting against the Muslim community)

Terrorism

Land, sea, or air piracy

Rape

Adultery

Homosexual behavior

Reasons for Capital Punishment in Islam

Capital punishment applies in the case of a person who meets any of the following conditions:

1 – The apostate. The apostate is one who disbelieves after being a Muslim, because the Prophet (peace and blessings of Allah be upon him) said: "Whoever changes his religion, execute him" (narrated by al-Bukhaari, 6524).

2 – The married adulterer. The punishment in this case is to be stoned to death. *Al-muhsan*, or the married person, here means one who got married and had intercourse with his wife in the vagina, in a legitimate marriage in which both parties are free, of sound mind and adults. If a married man or woman commits adultery, then they are to be stoned to death, because the Prophet (peace and blessings of Allah be upon him) said: "Learn from me. Allah has given them a way out. If an unmarried person commits fornication with an unmarried person, (the punishment is) one hundred lashes and exile for one

year. If a married person commits adultery with a married person, (the punishment is) one hundred lashes and stoning" (narrated by Muslim, 1690).

The Messenger of Allah (S) said: 'By the One in Whose hand is my soul, I will judge between you according to the Book of Allah. The offspring and sheep will be returned (i.e., there is no ransom), and your son is to be given one hundred lashes and exiled for one year. O Unays [who was one of the Sahaabah], go tomorrow to that woman and if she admits (this crime) then stone her.' So, he went to her the next day and she admitted it, and the Messenger of Allah (peace and blessings of Allah be upon him) issued orders that she be stoned.

3 – The murderer (one who kills deliberately). He is to be killed in retaliation (qisaas) unless the victim's next of kin let him off or agree to accept the diyah (blood money), because Allah says (interpretation of the meaning):

"O you who believe! Al-Qisaas (the Law of Equality in Punishment) is prescribed for you in case of murder: the free for the free, the slave for the slave, and the female for the female. But if the killer is forgiven by the brother (or the relatives) of the killed against blood money, then adhering to it with fairness and payment of the blood money to the heir should be made in fairness. This is an alleviation and a mercy from your Lord. So, after this whoever transgresses the limits (i.e. kills the killer after taking the blood money), he shall have a painful torment."

And the Prophet (peace and blessings of Allah be upon him) said: "It is not permissible (to shed) the blood of a Muslim who bears witness that there is no god but Allah and that I am the Messenger of Allah, except in three cases: a married adulterer, a soul for a soul, or one who leaves the religion and splits from the congregation" (narrated by al-Bukhari, 6484; Muslim, 1676).

4 – Bandits, i.e., *al-muhaarib*, those who wage war against Allah and His Messenger. Allah says (interpretation of the meaning):

"The recompense of those who wage war against Allah and His Messenger and do mischief in the land is only that they shall be killed or crucified or their hands and their feet be cut off from opposite sides, or be exiled from the land. That is their disgrace in this world, and a great torment is theirs in the Hereafter" *[al-Maa'idah 5:33]*.

5 – Those who spy on the Muslims and transmit information to their enemies.

The evidence for that is the report narrated by al-Bukhaari (3007) and Muslim (2494) which says that Haatib ibn Abi Balta'ah wrote to some of the mushrikeen in Makkah telling them some information about the Messenger of Allah (peace and blessings of Allah be upon him). The Messenger of Allah (peace and blessings of Allah be upon him) said: "O Haatib, what is this?" He said, "O Messenger of Allah, do not hasten to judge me. I was a man closely connected to Quraysh, but I did not belong to this tribe, while the other Muhaajireen with you had their relatives in Makkah who would protect their families and property. So, I wanted to make up for my lack of blood ties to them by doing them a favor so that they might protect my family. I did not do this because of disbelief or apostasy nor out of preferring kufr (disbelief) to Islam." The Messenger of Allaah (peace and blessings of Allah be upon him) said, "He has told you the truth." Umar said, "O Messenger of Allaah! Let me chop off the head of this hypocrite!" The Messenger of Allah (peace and blessings of Allah be upon him) said: "He was present at the battle of Badr, and you do not know, perhaps Allah looked at the people of Badr and said, 'Do whatever you like, for I have forgiven you.'"

The point in this hadeeth is that the Prophet (peace and blessings of Allah be upon him) agreed with 'Umar that Haatib deserved to be executed for this action, but the Prophet (peace and blessings of Allah be upon him) told him that there was a reason why he should not be killed, which is that he was one of those who was present at the battle of Badr.

Ibn al-Qayyim said in *Zaad al-Ma'aad* (2/115), concerning the hadeeth of Haatib ibn Abi Balta'ah:

This was quoted as evidence by those who do not think that the Muslim spy should be killed, such as al-Shaafa'i, Ahmad and Abu Haneefah (may Allaah have mercy on them). And it was quoted as evidence by those who think that the spy should be killed, such as Maalik and Ibn 'Aqeel among the companions of Ahmad, and others. They said: This is because the reason for not killing him was that he had been present at Badr. If being Muslim was the reason for not killing him, he would not have given a reason that is more specific, which is the fact that he had been present at Badr.

And he said elsewhere in *Zaad al-Ma'aad* (3/422):

The correct view is that execution of a spy depends on the opinion of the ruler; if executing him is in the Muslims' interests, he should be executed, but if letting him live serves a greater interest, then he should be allowed to live. And Allaah knows best.

The above also includes the one who does not pray, the one who practices witchcraft, and the heretic, because they fall under the heading of "the one who leaves his religion and splits from the jamaa'ah."

With regard to the conditions of implementing this punishment, there are many. Each crime has its own specific conditions, details of which may be found in the books of fiqh.

Methods of Capital Punishment

Actual methods of capital punishment vary from place to place. In some Muslim countries, methods have included beheading, hanging, stoning, and death by firing squad.

Executions are held publicly in Muslim countries, a tradition that is intended to warn would-be criminals.

Although Islamic justice is often criticized by other nations, it is important to note that there is no place for vigilantism in Islam. One must be properly convicted in an Islamic court of law before the punishment can be meted out. The severity of the punishment requires that very strict evidence standards must be met before a conviction is found. The court also has the flexibility to order less than the ultimate punishment (for example, imposing fines or prison sentences), on a case-by-case basis, e.g. blood money (*Diyyah*).

Blood Money (*Diyyah*)

In Islamic law, victims of crime are recognized as having rights. The victim has a say in how the criminal is to be punished. In general, Islamic law calls for murderers to face the death penalty. However, the victim's next of kin may choose to excuse the murderer from the death penalty in exchange for monetary damages. The murderer will still be sentenced by a judge, possibly to a lengthy prison term, but the death penalty will be taken off the table.

This principle is known as *Diyyah*, which is unfortunately known in English as "blood money." It is more appropriately referred to as "victim's compensation." While most commonly associated with death penalty cases, *Diyyah* payments can also be made for lesser crimes and for acts of negligence (e.g. falling asleep at the wheel of a car and causing an accident). The concept is similar to the practice in many Western courts where the state prosecutor files a criminal case against the defendant, but the victim or family members may also sue in civil court for damages. However, in Islamic law, if the victim or victim's representatives accept monetary payment, it is considered an act of forgiveness which in turn lessens the criminal's penalty.

In the Quran, *Diyyah* is encouraged as a matter of forgiveness and to release people from the desire for vengeance. The Quran says:

Oh, you who believe! The law of equality is prescribed to you in cases of murder... but if any remission is made by the brother of the slain, then grant any reasonable demand, and compensate him with handsome gratitude. This is a concession and a Mercy from your Lord. After this whoever exceeds the limits shall be in grave penalty. In the Law of Equality there is (saving of) life to you, oh men of understanding; that you may restrain yourselves. (2:178-179)

Never should a believer kill a believer, but if it so happens by mistake, compensation is due. If one so kills a believer, it is ordained that he should free a believing slave, and pay compensation to the deceased's family, unless they remit it freely.... If he (the deceased) belonged to a people with whom you have treaty of mutual alliance, compensation should be paid to his family, and a believing slave be freed. For those who find this beyond their means, is prescribed a fast for two months running, by way of repentance to Allah, for Allah has all knowledge and all wisdom. (4:92)

There is no set price in Islam for the amount of *Diyyah* payment. It is often left to negotiation, but in some Muslim countries there are minimum amounts set by law. If the accused cannot afford the payment, the extended family or state will often step in to help. In some Muslim countries, there are charitable funds set aside strictly for this purpose.

There is also no standard with regard to the amount for men vs. women, Muslim vs. non-Muslim, and so on. The minimum amounts set by law in some countries do distinguish based on gender, allowing double the amount for a male victim over a female victim. This is generally understood to be related to the amount of potential future earnings lost from that family member. In some Bedouin cultures, however, the amount for a female victim could be up to six times greater than that of a male victim.

Debate

Although capital punishment is still widely supported in Islamic states and nations in which Islam is the state religion, there are growing groups of Muslims that support the abolishment of the death penalty. Those who oppose capital punishment disagree with the mainstream interpretation of Quran passages regarding capital punishment.

The implementation of capital punishment for crimes other than murder is a different standard than that used elsewhere in the world. Defenders can argue that the Islamic practice does serve as a deterrent and that Muslim countries are less troubled by the routine social violence that plagues some other societies as a result of their legal strictness.

In Muslim countries with stable governments, for example, murder rates are relatively low. Detractors would argue that Islamic law borders on the barbaric for imposing death sentences on so-called victimless crimes such as adultery or homosexual behavior.

Debate on this issue is ongoing and not likely to be resolved in the near future.

Buddhism and the Death Penalty

On September 21, 2011, the state of Georgia took Troy Davis's life, despite a lack of evidence proving his guilt. On the same day, the white supremacist Lawrence Brewer was killed by lethal injection by the state of Texas, despite the request by the victim's family that the district attorney not seek the death penalty. The state of Florida later witnessed the execution of Manuel Valle on September 28, the same year after he spent 33 years on death row.

Buddhists, along with a growing number of members of other religions, believe that the death penalty is fundamentally unethical. From the Buddhist perspective, non-violence, or not harming others, is the heart of the Buddha's teachings.

The core philosophies of Buddhism contradict capital punishment. Buddhists follow five precepts, or rules, about actions to avoid. The first of these precepts specifically prohibits harming or killing any living thing. Buddhists attempt to lead a life that causes the least amount of harm possible; executing even people who are guilty of heinous crimes defies this concept. The Buddha taught followers to return acts of evil with acts of compassion, which further contradicts the death penalty.

Buddhists perceive any intense punishment as detrimental not only to the recipient, but to the executioner as well. While Buddhism philosophically opposes the death penalty, some countries with significant Buddhist populations still practice it as of 2013; Thailand is such an example.

Everyone has the ability to uproot negative, self-centred thoughts and instead nourish an open engagement with others. In doing so, we find true happiness and fulfil our potential as human beings.

Manuel Valle, Troy Davis, and Lawrence Brewer and the 3,200 inmates on death row will not have this opportunity.

According to Buddhism, everything that happens in our lives is the result of causes and conditions. Nothing happens at random. Every action gives rise to results that we experience immediately or in the future. By not committing any of the five non-virtuous actions (killing, lying, stealing, sexual misconduct, taking intoxicants), we ensure that we ourselves are not victims of murder, theft, etc. Likewise, when we do experience such misfortunes, we recognize that they arise in our lives only because of similar actions we committed in the past. We bear full responsibility for our present and future lives, both for the positive and negative experiences.

The religion believes fundamentally in the cycle of birth and re-birth (Samsara) and teaches that if capital punishment is administered it will have compromising effects on the souls of both the offender and the punisher in future incarnations.

As far as punishment in this world is concerned, Buddhism has strong views:

Inhumane treatment of an offender does not solve their misdeeds or those of humanity in general. The best approach to an offender is reformatory rather than punitive.

Punishment should only be to the extent to which the offender needs to make amends, and his rehabilitation into society should be of paramount importance.

Punishing an offender with excessive cruelty will injure not just the offender's mind, but also the mind of the person doing the punishing.

It is impossible to administer severe punishment with composure and compassion.

If the crime is particularly serious, the person may be banished from the community or country.

In the works of a great Tibetan scholar, the Sakya Pandita, "Howsoever anyone breaks the law, they may win for a while, but in the end, they lose." Even though someone may appear to get away with breaking the law, in the long run, he/she will experience the results of the negative action. Karma, the law of cause and effect, is definite and not subject to the inequities and arbitrariness of any legal system. As such, the death penalty is unnecessary, because the person who violates the law by committing murder will definitely bear the horrible, irreversible karmic consequences.

In the *Dhammapada,* we find the following verses:

Whoever harms with violence those who are gentle and innocent, to one of these ten states that person quickly descends:

he would beget severe suffering; deprivation and fracturing of the body; or grave illness, too; mental imbalance; trouble from the government; cruel slander; loss of relatives; or obstruction of property.

One of the principle teachings of Buddhism is showing compassion toward others. While Buddhists acknowledge that all life involves suffering, they seek to find a means of ending the suffering. Showing compassion towards fellow humans, which includes showing mercy to people who have done wrong, helps Buddhists develop spiritually. The Buddha advocates expressing mercy towards others, and instead of wishing enemies or wrongdoers ill, they wish them well. Their meditation of loving-kindness involves one stage in which people meditating wish love unto someone who they dislike.

Buddhism opposes any severe punishment, as Buddhists see it as an affront to both the recipient and the person conducting the punishment. A person is incapable of delivering any extreme punishment with compassion, a trait that all Buddhists must show to all living things. The aim of punishment, to them, should not be retribution but rehabilitation; it should help a person grow and recover to better fit into society. In the most extreme cases, people can be banished from the town or city if there is no hope of rehabilitation.

However, despite the Buddhists' opposition to cruel punishment and their support to showing mercy to others, they do not feel that people can act in any way they wish without consequences. Instead, they believe that people's actions will result in either positive or negative consequences in the future. This is a concept known as *karma*. Buddhism instructs followers to avoid things like killing, lying, stealing, and consuming drugs and alcohol because of the belief that if a person lives an immoral life, they will receive bad actions returning to them: if people have bad karma in this life, it extends to the next life.

Both murderers and supporters of the death penalty deserve our compassion because they will experience the karmic effects of killing. It may seem strange to generate compassion towards those who harm us. Buddha taught that our actions are influenced by causes and conditions; similarly, our minds are poisoned by ignorance, attachment and hatred. When our minds are overcome by hatred, at that moment, we go crazy, and we are not able to control ourselves.

It is interesting to note that despite these teachings, several countries with substantial Buddhist populations retain the death penalty, and some of them, for example Thailand, continue to use it. Alarid and Wang, in *Mercy and Punishment: Buddhism and the Death Penalty*, suggest that this apparent paradox partly stems from the difference between popular and monastic Buddhism. The majority of lay Buddhists in these countries follow Buddhist practices and are entirely sincere in their commitment, but "the genuine study of Buddhism, its rituals, and carryover to daily life is superficial for most Buddhist followers."

According to the authors, other reasons Buddhist countries retain the death penalty are:

Belief by politicians that capital punishment is necessary for retribution, cultural customs, or for deterrence value.

A long tradition of capital punishment in a particular country.

Keeping order in society is seen as more important than Buddha's teaching.

Reaction to long periods of political unrest or economic instability.

Moralistic Views on the Use of Capital Punishment

According to a recent survey found on www.pollingreport.com, most people in the U.S. today favor the death penalty and appear to be reasonably satisfied with the number of executions that take place, as reflected in the results given below:

"Do you believe in capital punishment -- that is, the death penalty -- or are you opposed to it?" (2/5-11/08)
Believe in It: 63

Opposed: 30

Unsure: 7

"Do you feel that executing people who commit murder deters others from committing murder, or do

you think such executions don't have much effect?"
(2/5-11/08)

Deters Others: 42

Not Much Effect: 52

Unsure: 6

"In general, would you like to see an increase or decrease in the number of convicted criminals who are executed, or no change?" (2/5-11/08)

Increase: 36

Decrease: 26

No Change: 31

Unsure: 7

"Do you think that innocent people are sometimes convicted of murder, or that this never happens?"
(2/5-11/08)

Sometimes: 95

Never: 4

Unsure: 1

With the increase in the rate of the use of the death penalty as a form of punishment for crimes committed in some countries, the support shown for this otherwise brutal form of punishment, and the continuous cry of international communities on the need to completely abolish this act, a lot has been written on the debate on whether executing criminals is ever a morally defensible form of punishment or not. This section will examine the five major traditional justifications used in support of this act, these are: retribution, the social contract, rights forfeiture, utilitarianism and social benefit as explained by James Fieser in *Moral Issues that Divide Us.*

Retribution

The first traditional justification of the death penalty is that it is a direct application of the retributive conception of punishment: The death penalty is justified as a proportionate punishment for a serious crime, which should be carried out because it is deserved for its own sake, and not because of any benefit that it might bring to society. The oldest example of this is the "eye for an eye" principle of retaliation, which when applied to murder means "a life for a life".

'Bad guys deserve to suffer' is a blunt slogan that aptly captures the essence of a deeply familiar notion: People who have committed culpable wrongs deserve their lives to be worse as a result. Why do they deserve it? Perhaps because it is not fair for the lives of wrongdoers to go well when the lives of the innocent have gone poorly- punishment levels the playing field.

Retributivists argue that the punishment of criminals is intrinsically valuable. Even if punishing murderers and thieves had no effect on reducing the overall crime rate, retributivists tend to think it is still the right thing to do. They also think that the severity of punishment should match the severity of the crime. So just as it is wrong to over-punish someone (executing for stealing clothes), it can also be wrong to under-punish someone (giving someone community service for murder).

Advocates of retributivist capital punishment, past or present, do not often explain the moral foundation of the "eye for an eye" principle of retaliation, or present any compelling argument. Instead, it is often appealed to as time-honored common sense or an article of religious faith. The idea has been with us for thousands of years and has become a normal part of our thinking when it comes to punishment. An important exception to this, however, is German philosopher Immanuel Kant (1724-1804) who offers a thoroughly original argument in its defense.

For Kant, the death penalty is grounded in the idea that every person is valuable and worthy of respect because of their ability to make rational and free choices. The murderer, too, is worthy of respect, and we consequently show him that respect by treating him the same way he declares that people are to be treated. Accordingly, we execute the murderer.

At first, Kant's theory seems backwards. Ordinarily we might think that murderers are worthless beasts, deserving of no dignity, and should therefore be executed. Kant, though, disagrees. If I, as a rational person, choose to behave towards you in a particular manner, I am declaring more generally that in my assessment this is how everyone should be treated, including myself. It is as though I am making a request whereby through my actions towards others, I tell others how I should be treated.

If I behave badly towards others, then that behavior should come right back on me in the form of a comparable punishment. I am deciding for myself how I am to be treated, and society is respecting my decision in how it reacts to my bad behavior. This, then, is what happens when people commit murder. Because every person is a valuable human being who is worthy of respect, including the murderer himself, the dignity of a murderer demands that he be executed. Kant writes,

The undeserved evil which any one commits on another, is to be regarded as perpetrated on himself. Hence it may be said: If you slander another, you slander yourself; if you steal from another, you steal from yourself; if you strike another, you strike yourself; if you kill another, you kill yourself. [The Philosophy of Law, 2.49.e.1]

Thus, according to Kant, whoever commits murder must die. However, his execution must be humane and as painless as possible: "His death must be kept free from all maltreatment that would make the humanity suffering in his person loathsome or abominable" (ibid). Kant's account of capital punishment is retributive insofar as society is merely giving the criminal what he deserves.

However, there are three problems with retributivist capital punishment, particularly when based on the "eye for an eye" principle. The first criticism is that a strict application of "eye for an eye" justice leads to counterintuitive judgements. As we have seen, in non-death penalty cases it leads to the troublesome judgement that arsonists should have their homes burned down or that rapists should be raped. This problem also applies to Kant's version: We do not punish an arsonist by burning down his house, even if that is how the arsonist himself deems that people should be treated. In death penalty cases, we find the same problem, such as this from Hammurabi: "If it kills the son of the owner, then the son of that builder shall be put to death" (230).

If this sentence was carried out, the pain of the builder would be parallel to the pain of the owner, but, at least by today's standards, the builder's son is an independent person from his father and killing him would be wrong. The problem is that mechanically applying the "eye for an eye" formula will not guarantee that the punishment will be always an appropriate or even logical one. If we did start out by using the formula, we would then need to make an independent moral judgment about whether that application of the formula was a good one. If we are then reliant upon that independent moral judgment for a proper assessment of a punishment, then the "eye for an eye" formula is not only unnecessary, but harmfully misleading. It distracts from the assessment of true justice and should be set aside.

The second criticism of retributivist capital punishment is that a strict application of the "eye for an eye" formula may even be inadequate. If a mass murderer kills ten people, then taking his single life is technically not punishment in kind. Think of how many times we would need to have executed Hitler to balance out the murders that he is responsible for. Some people are so bad that there is no way of retributively balancing the scales of justice. Part of the appeal of retributivism is that it makes punishments proportional to the crimes and thereby balances the scales. But this feature is lost with the worst criminals. Again, this problem also applies to Kant: even if Hitler proclaims through his conduct that this is the way people should be treated, a single death would be nowhere sufficient.

While these two criticisms of the eye for an eye principle seem persuasive enough, contemporary American philosopher Christopher Wellman is not so sure. Wellman states that he is "no cheerleader for the death penalty" and for at least practical reasons he would not support the idea of government officials "raping rapists or torturing torturers." However, he believes that the wrongness of doing so is not immediately evident from typical retributivist reasoning:

It is not clear how one could establish the unreasonableness of the claim that Hitler, for instance, forfeited his right not to be tortured to death. How can one rationally defeat the claim that the members of the paramilitary groups in the former Yugoslavia who engaged in mass rape as an element of their campaign of so-called ethnic cleansing forfeited their rights against being raped? [The Rights

Forfeiture Theory of Punishment Ethics, Vol. 122, 2012]

Some actions are so horrendous that balancing the scales of justice through "eye for an eye" retribution seems like a reasonable idea, and the examples that Wellman cites are good ones. Suppose, though, that we caught Hitler and brutally killed him the same way that he killed millions of people in death camps. It would quickly become evident that this punishment was woefully insufficient for balancing the scales of justice, and the punishment did not come close to fitting the crime. What then did we accomplish through our efforts? Probably not much more than the venting of our feelings of anger and vengeance towards Hitler, which, as we have seen earlier, is not what true retribution is about. That is, retribution is not about appeasing our negative feelings towards criminals, but carrying out what is deserved. Contrary to Wellman's observation, it is precisely cases like Hitler's that reveal the wrongness of torturing torturers, or raping rapists. Our "eye for an eye" response would not really be about justice, but about our vengeful retaliation, and thus not in the spirit of true retribution.

There is yet a third criticism of the strict "eye for an eye" punishment which may be even more damaging than the first two. Society has in fact already moved beyond strict "eye for an eye" punishment for less serious crimes, and this suggests that it is also time to do so with murder. The Law of Hammurabi reveals a time in human history when the "eye for an eye" formula was applied to many crimes. It may have been too severe by our standards, but it at least it attempted to formulate a consistent system of justice. Sections 191-282 of Hammurabi lay out appropriate punishments for crimes. Several follow the strict "eye for an eye" formula, such as a broken bone for a broken bone, and a knocked-out tooth for a knocked-out tooth. Others follow it only symbolically, such as cutting off the tongue of a son who denounces his father, or the fingers of a son who hits his father.

When evaluating acceptable forms of punishment, one Supreme Court justice famously referred to "evolving standards of decency that mark the progress of a maturing society," where some types of punishment can be "more primitive than torture" (Trop v. Dulles). One indication of this evolution is how far we have moved away from the Law of Hammurabi, with the last vestige being the "eye for an eye" justification of capital punishment. It may be time to abandon this rationale as a relic from a less civilized period of human history.

If we do set aside the strict application of "eye for an eye" justice, what then remains of the retributive justification of capital punishment? Not much, since retributivism would no longer require the death penalty in cases of murder. The larger retributivist intuition is an important and indispensable one, namely, that criminals should be punished as deserved, and the scales of justice need to be balanced. To accomplish this, we need to make a moral assessment about what would count as adequate compensation for a crime. Maybe that assessment would lead to the conclusion that the death penalty is deserved, but, without the strict "eye for an eye" formula, it is not necessarily required, since other types of adequate compensation are available, particularly long-term imprisonment.

Rights Forfeiture

A second traditional justification of the death penalty is that when people commit serious crimes, they forfeit their right to life, and thus may be executed. The concept of rights forfeiture is frequently appealed to as a justification for other forms of punishment, such as imprisonment. If you commit a violent crime, you forfeit your liberty rights, and society may place you in prison where you no longer have the freedom of movement and expression.

The idea of rights forfeiture was first articulated by British philosopher John Locke (1632-1704), who argued that from birth I have natural God-given rights to life, health, liberty and property. I retain these rights throughout my life, Locke says, unless I violate the fundamental rights of others, in which case I enter a condition of war with my victim, and I forfeit my right to life. This entitles my victim to kill me, just as he would be entitled to kill a dangerous animal that threatened him. Locke argues,

For man, not having such an arbitrary power over his own life, cannot give another man such a power over it, but it is the effect only of forfeiture which the aggressor makes of his own life when he puts himself into the state of war with another. For having quitted reason . . . he renders himself liable to be destroyed by his adversary whenever he can, as any other noxious and brutish creature that is destructive to his being. [Second Treatise on Government, 172]

Locke held that I forfeit my right to life not only if I attempt to murder someone, but also if I forcibly rob someone, even when I have no intention of killing my victim. This is because I have my victim within my power when I take his possessions, and my victim can reasonably assume that, when he is under my power, I will "take away everything else," including his life. From Locke's time onward, rights forfeiture has been a popular reason given in support of capital punishment. At the same time, though, it has been persistently criticized, and we will consider two recurring objections.

The major criticism of this justification is that rights forfeiture allows for vigilantism: if I forfeit my life by killing someone, then anyone may hunt me down and kill me. We presume that only the state has the authority to do so, but if I am now without any right to life because of my violent conduct, then my life is in a sense part of the public domain and free for the taking by anyone, not just the state.

Clearly, this is an unsustainable position. We in fact do not permit vigilantism and, more importantly, we believe that vigilantism is wrong. Rather, we believe that the authority to carry out executions must rest within the state, not within private initiative. Thus, the theory of rights forfeiture is inherently flawed. While Locke did not directly address this issue, there is enough in his political theory to develop a plausible response to this problem of vigilantism.

For Locke, rights forfeiture is built into the very concept of natural rights as devised by God (or, alternatively, by nature), who also made the rules and conditions of natural rights. If I am living in a pre-society natural condition and I attempt to kill someone, then, according to the rules of natural rights, I forfeit my right to life specifically to my victim, who in turn has the authority to kill me. At best, it is only my victim, and by extension his family or associates acting on his behalf, that have the right to vigilante justice. But even that right to vigilantism is short-lived.

Once societies are established, we hand over our right to vigilante justice to the state, and governments then have the sole authority to execute the aggressor. We add a layer of civility over top of the rights that we have in a natural condition, and, in the interest of law and order, give up some of the freedoms that we previously had. Thus, within Locke's theory, we can find a plausible response to this first criticism.

According to Fieser, a second criticism of rights forfeiture is that it is inherently at odds with the concept of rights inalienability, which most generally means that rights cannot be given up. The notion of inalienability is a fuzzy one that is open to interpretation, and the tension between forfeiture and inalienability emerges if we make a distinction between what we may call "weak" inalienability and "strong" inalienability:

• *Weak inalienability*: An inalienable right is one that may not be voluntarily relinquished or transferred by the right-holder, but may be forfeited by the right-holder by committing a crime.

• *Strong inalienability*: An inalienable right is one that may not be separated from the right-holder for any reason whatever.

On these definitions, weak inalienability is compatible with rights forfeiture, but strong inalienability is incompatible with it. The intuition behind weak inalienability is that liberty rights, such as the right of free movement, are forfeitable if I commit a crime like theft and am locked up in prison as a punishment. The same can be said if I commit murder and am executed as a punishment.

In each case, the rights are both inalienable and forfeitable. By contrast, the intuition behind strong inalienability is that the right to life is completely non-negotiable, regardless of what crimes we may have committed. If I commit theft, I still retain my liberty rights, although the government can justly restrict my exercise of it by putting me in prison. It is like the way your boss restricts your liberty to wander around the office building when you should be at your desk.

However, if I commit murder, I still retain my right to life, but the government cannot execute me since this would annihilate my right to life, not merely restrict it.

They can still restrict my liberty by putting me in prison for murder, but the idea of a right to life is not meaningful if it can have exceptions here and there. It is, instead, exception-less.

Locke himself does not use the expression "inalienable right", which was only introduced a half-century after him and quickly attained an almost magical significance by Jefferson in the Declaration of Independence. But Locke does advocate the key features of weak inalienability in his account of rights theory. According to him, even though I might forfeit my right to life to someone that I attack, I still cannot voluntarily transfer that right over to someone, such as by selling myself into slavery:

A man, not having the power of his own life, cannot, by compact, or his own consent, enslave himself to any one, nor put himself under the absolute, arbitrary power of another, to take away his life, when he pleases. Nobody can give more power than he has himself; and he that cannot take away his own life, cannot give another power over it. [Second Treatise on Government, 23]

Even though Locke sides with weak inalienability, not everyone after him did. Accordingly, defenders of capital punishment held to weak inalienability, and critics of it held to the strong version. Here are short examples of each from nineteenth-century writers on the subject:

Pro capital punishment (weak inalienability): "Is not liberty and every other right as inalienable as that of life? . . . If the murderer takes the life of his brother, you say he does not forfeit his own. We ask then, does he forfeit his liberty? Does he forfeit anything?" [Plummer, *Defence of Capital Punishment*, 1846]

Contra capital punishment (strong inalienability): "Opponents [of the death penalty] stand on the admitted general rule that human life is sacred; or, as it is stated in our national declaration, that the right to life is among the 'inalienable rights' with which 'all men are endowed by their Creator'." [Burleigh, *Thoughts on the Death Penalty*, 1847]

So, does rights forfeiture succeed as a justification for capital punishment? That depends. Rights theory is a flexible notion that, with enough creativity, can be shaped in different ways. If it is formulated in a way that accepts weak inalienability, then, yes, it may justify capital punishment. However, if it is formulated differently so that it accepts strong inalienability, then, no, it does not justify capital punishment.

This flexibility of rights theory, where it might be formulated in either direction, raises a red flag. It would be nice if we could know the exact features of rights, but unfortunately there is no universal consensus about exactly which rights we have, which beings or entities have rights, and whether forfeiture or inalienability are part of the rights package. Because of this, we often bend rights theory to support our own moral convictions, rather than consult it as an impartial tool for determining what is right or wrong, just or unjust. This seems to be the case when examining the morality of capital punishment, and, as such, rights theory is not much help.

Social Contract

The third traditional defense of the death penalty is that it is justified through the social contract: To preserve the peace, citizens contractually agree to set aside their hostilities and set up a government that will punish lawbreakers, including executing them if deemed necessary.

As Thomas Hobbes describes the situation, prior to the creation of governments, humans lived in a hostile natural condition in which we competed for survival, which made our lives "solitary, nasty, brutish and short." Our natural desire for a long and productive life motivates us to seek the best means of living peacefully with our fellow humans, and the social contract is the mechanism to accomplish this. According to Hobbes, for the government to effectively ensure that citizens abide by the terms of the contract, it must have the authority to punish criminals who break the rules, and sometimes this requires capital punishment.

So far, this social contract justification of capital punishment sounds reasonable, considering that the alternative is to have society collapse, which would throw us back into a state of nature. But Hobbes himself points out two problems with justifying the death penalty through the social contract.

First, my purpose for entering into the contract to begin with is to preserve my life, and, thus, it is contrary to that purpose if I agree to a death penalty for myself. He writes that "No man is obliged by any contracts whatsoever not to resist him who shall offer to kill, wound, or any other way hurt his body" (*De Civi*, 18). Hobbes's solution to this problem is that I may accept a contract that permits the government to *attempt* to kill me if I commit a serious crime, but I cannot accept a contract that requires me to passively *allow* the government to kill me. The most that I can do is agree to not help some other criminal escape punishment, but I am entitled to do everything that I can to escape punishment for myself.

The second problem with justifying capital punishment through the social contract concerns how the government got permission to kill us to begin with. If the contract stipulates that we all need to relinquish our rights to kill each other, then this should apply to the government too. Hobbes's solution is that the government did not sign that version of the contract. Imagine that you and I agree to get along with each other, but, to guarantee this, we hire a bully to beat us up if we break our agreement. The bully himself, though, is not part of that agreement, but only part of a different agreement that gives him policing powers over us. Similarly, the government is not part of the same contract that you and I are, and, technically speaking, the government is still in the warring state of nature and can kill whomever it wants. Rather, the government agreed to a different contract by which we give it the authority to police us, even under threat of the death penalty. Hobbes writes, "The subjects did not give the sovereign that right" to punish us by death, but, instead, it is a right that it still has from the state of nature (*Leviathan*, 28).

Thus, Hobbes's version of social contract theory does justify capital punishment, but only barely so, and in a convoluted way. We find a much tidier justification of the death penalty by French philosopher Jean Jacques Rousseau (1712–1778) who argued that, when signing the social contract, I am indeed agreeing to allow the government to execute me if I interfere with the larger social good. Rousseau raises the problem that first bothered Hobbes: How can individuals, who have no right to dispose of their own lives, transfer to the government a right which they do not possess? Rousseau's answer is that I am entitled to put my life at risk for the prospect of achieving a better situation for myself, and people do this all the time. To avoid being burned in a fire, I may rightfully jump out a window even if it results in my death. If I need to make an important trip when the travelling conditions are dangerous, I am entitled to do that too. For Rousseau, the situation is the same when we sign the

social contract:

The social treaty has for its end the preservation of the contracting parties. He who wills the end wills the means also, and the means must involve some risks, and even some losses. He who wishes to preserve his life at others' expense should also, when it is necessary, be ready to give it up for their sake. [The Social Contract, 2.5]

By signing the social contract, I take on the risk that the government may judge my actions to be criminal and execute me. But it is a risk that I am willing to take since the rewards of living in a peaceful society are worth it, especially considering that the alternative is to live a miserable life outside of society.

Rousseau's reasoning is more straightforward than Hobbes's, and has become the standard social contract justification of capital punishment. It is also Rousseau's version that critics of the death penalty attack. We see this first with Beccaria, who argued that no one would ever agree to give up his right to life as a requirement for entering society: "Each person gives only the smallest portion of his liberty over to the good of the public. Is it possible that this small portion [of liberty] contains the greatest good of all, namely, that person's life?" (*On Crimes and Punishment*, 28).

I may agree to the idea of forfeiting some of my rights if I violate the law, if that is what is needed to become a member of society. I may be willing to risk jail time for the benefits of living within a peaceful and well governed society. However, it is not reasonable for me to risk being executed to receive society's benefits. The whole point of entering society is to get some benefit, and I get no such benefit if I am dead.

Beccaria provided only a short critique of Rousseau's position, but a more detailed one was offered by American statesman Robert Rantoul (1805-1852). It is not reasonable, he argues, that we consented to place our lives "at the discretion, or the caprice of a majority, whose erratic legislation no man can calculate beforehand." Rantoul cites the French Revolution itself as an example, when, during the Reign of Terror, 17,000 people were executed, with its leaders using Rousseau's social contract theory as philosophical defense.

Further, he argues, considering how zealously the government protects the rights of property, liberty and personal security, it makes no sense that the government should so easily discard the right to life. Finally, Rantoul argues that no reason can be given why a person would trade in his right to life under one social contract system, when under a different social contract, he could retain the right to life while still receiving the necessary benefits of a government:

Let there, at least, be shown some reason for supposing that any sane man has of his own accord bartered away his original right in his own existence, that his government may tyrannize more heavily over him and his fellows, when all the purposes of good government may be amply secured at so much cheaper a purchase. In no instance can this preposterous sacrifice be implied. [Report on the Abolition of Capital Punishment, 1836]

While Rousseau's social contract defense of capital punishment is simple and organized, it now seems almost naive in the face of Beccaria's and Rantoul's criticisms. There is no obvious reason why we should willingly hand our right to life over to an impulsive and unpredictable government when we might obtain comparable security from an alternative government without relinquishing that right.

If capital punishment can be reasonably defended by social contract theory, it may be only through a complicated one like Hobbes's. The effect of Hobbes's account is that, when no better alternative is available, yes, we will sign a social contract that is managed by a bully who might impose the death penalty, but if it ever comes to that, we do not have to cooperate with the bully and passively accept our death.

Utilitarianism

The fourth traditional defense of capital punishment is that society is better off with it than without it. This approach is sometimes called the argument from "expediency", but the rationale is most associated with utilitarian philosophers.

Utilitarianism is a general moral philosophy that holds that an action is morally right if the consequences of that action are more favorable than unfavorable to everyone. In determining whether capital punishment is morally justified, then, we need to consider both the beneficial and harmful consequences of it: if it is generally more beneficial than it is permissible, if not then it is impermissible.

The utilitarian approach to capital punishment substantially differs from those that have been examined so far. Considerations about retribution, the social contract and rights forfeiture are based largely on foundational ideological convictions, with minimal emphasis on whether capital punishment in fact will improve the world. The utilitarian approach to capital punishment, though, is all about gathering facts and performing a cost-benefit analysis to determine whether the death penalty will indeed make the world a better place.

Jeremy Bentham (1748-1832), who was among the classic utilitarian philosophers, produced the most systematic analysis of capital punishment. At the time Bentham wrote, English law had the enormous number of capital offenses noted earlier, and this factored into his analysis. Below is a summary of his list of both the advantages and disadvantages of the death penalty, which includes special disadvantages of capital punishment for minor crimes.

Advantages of Capital Punishment

- It is similar to the offense in cases of murder (i.e., a death for a death).
- It has popular appeal in cases of murder.
- It prevents criminals from repeating their crimes.
- It deters others by making a lasting impression on them.

Disadvantages of Capital Punishment

- I t eliminates any restitution or special service that the criminal might perform.
- It creates a financial loss to society by permanently removing criminals from the work force.
- It is not a heavy punishment to criminals who have little to live for.
- It is irreversible in cases of error.

Special Disadvantages of Capital Punishment for Minor Crimes

- It makes perjury appear meritorious when compassionate judges intentionally undervalue the cost of stolen items.
- It produces a general disrespect for the law since such a small percentage of convicted criminals receive the full sentence.
- It makes convictions arbitrary and pardons necessary.

    [paraphrased from Bentham, *Rationale of Punishment*, 1775, 12]

Bentham's final assessment is that capital punishment has more disadvantages than advantages, and, thus, it should be abolished for all crimes.

Regarding his list of advantages of capital punishment, he has a criticism of each one. First, concerning the analogy of a death for a death, Bentham states that "analogy is a very good recommendation, but not a good justification." That is, it is an initially plausible suggestion since the punishment would be proportional to the crime, but further reasons would be needed to implement it. We have seen this in our analysis of "eye for an eye" retributivism above.

Second, regarding the popularity of capital punishment in murder cases, he argues that "Every other mode of punishment that is seen to be equally or more efficacious will become equally or more popular". He also argues that the current popularity of the death penalty can be explained by the desire for vengeance among citizens, and the deficiency of prisons to hold criminals (*On Death Punishment*, 1831).

Thirdly, Bentham considers the commonly held view that capital punishment is absolutely necessary in cases of murder, since it is believed that this is the only way to ensure that the criminal will not murder again. However, he argues, we will find that this assertion is "extremely exaggerated" when considering how we punish murderers who are insane:

It is never thought necessary that madmen should be put to death. They are not put to death: they are only kept in confinement; and that confinement is found effectually to answer the purpose. [Bentham, 1775]

This is all the more telling, he argues, since insane murders act arbitrarily and are thus more dangerous than murderers who kill merely for money and only do so when they believe that their crimes will go undetected. The fourth and final advantage of the death penalty that Bentham evaluates is that it deters others from committing crimes. Yes, he says, it "is true with respect to the majority of mankind: it is not true with respect to the greatest criminals". Criminals, he argues, lack the discipline and desire to obtain a living through consistent employment, and consequently "look upon the pleasures to be obtained by honest industry as not worth living for."

The only pleasures that they enjoy are those attainable through crime. Further, "their very [criminal] profession leads them continually to put their existence in jeopardy" and life itself does not have the same appeal to the criminal as it does for the noncriminal. Consequently, these criminals will be deterred more by the threat of permanent imprisonment in a structured work environment than they will by the death penalty.

Again, Bentham's conclusion is that the disadvantages of capital punishment far outweigh the advantages, and thus capital punishment should be abolished. But that is the analysis of just one utilitarian philosopher. Utilitarian approaches to moral decision making do not necessarily come with fixed judgments about any issue, whether it is capital punishment, sexual morality, or euthanasia, just to name a few. Instead, utilitarianism simply offers a formula for solving moral problems once we supply the relevant facts. British utilitarian philosopher John Stuart Mill (1806–1873) also examined the issue of capital punishment and arrived at a different conclusion: The death penalty is justified because of its deterrence value. Like Bentham, Mill argues that to the criminal himself, the death penalty may not seem as severe as permanent imprisonment:

What comparison can there really be, in point of severity, between consigning a man to the short pang of a rapid death, and immuring him in a living tomb, there to linger out what may be a long life in the hardest and most monotonous toil, without any of its alleviations or rewards [Speech before Parliament, April 21, 1868]

Capital punishment, then, is more merciful to the criminal than the alternative. Further, Mill continues, to the outsider, the death penalty is much more horrifying than permanent imprisonment, and thus makes a stronger and more lasting impression. For Mill, then, the formula is simple: the death penalty is less painful to the criminal and has greater deterrence on the public, whereas imprisonment is more painful to the criminal and has lesser deterrence on the public.

Accordingly, Mill concludes that he defends the death penalty "when confined to atrocious cases, on the very ground on which it is commonly attacked -- on that of humanity to the criminal; as beyond comparison the least cruel mode in which it is possible adequately to deter from the crime." Between Bentham and Mill, then, the utilitarian question of capital punishment comes down to its level of deterrence. It is not merely utilitarian philosophers who examine the deterrence value of the death penalty, but much of the debate today focuses on just that question, which we turn to next.

Deterrence

As we have seen from the utilitarian discussion, the question of capital punishment and deterrence is not whether the death penalty has any deterrent value at all, for it undoubtedly does. Rather, it is a question of whether executing criminals does a better job at deterring others than does long-term or permanent imprisonment.

Common sense suggests that the death penalty should be more effective. A parking fine of $100 will do a better job of deterring me from illegal parking than a mere fine of $10. Imagine how much more I would be deterred if the penalty for illegal parking was the death penalty; I might give up driving altogether. As compelling as this intuition might seem, there are other psychological factors at play. Beccaria argued that in time we will naturally grow accustomed to increases in severity of punishment, and consequently the initial increase in severity will lose its effect:

In proportion as punishments become crueller, the minds of people grow hardened and insensible; this is just as a fluid rises to the same height with that which surrounds it. And because of the continual force of the passions, in a period of a hundred years, the wheel terrifies no more than the prison did before. [On Crimes and Punishments, 27]

Thus, over time we would get used to the idea of the death penalty, and it would deter us no more than we previously would have been deterred by life imprisonment. The burden of proof, then, seems to be on the defender of capital punishment to show that the same deterrent effects could not be accomplished with a less severe punishment of long-term or life imprisonment.

How, though, might a defender of the death penalty demonstrate that it really does have greater deterrence value? Ideally, a truly scientific study of the question would involve a comparison between two otherwise identical societies in which capital punishment was not used in the control group, but was used in the test group.

The problem, though, is that it is a practical impossibility to isolate two otherwise identical societies upon which to conduct the study. There would be an almost endless variety of differing factors in the respective groups, such as differing rates of unemployment, drug use, education, gun ownership, church attendance, single parenthood, and gang membership.

In the absence of being able to conduct a scientifically perfect experiment to test the deterrence value of capital punishment, researchers have tried other approaches. A common method is to compare the murder rates of states that have the death penalty to those that do not. Another is to compare whether murder rates have increased or decreased when those same states have increased or decreased the number of executions.

Again, though, it is nearly impossible to remove the impact of other influences such as cultural and economic ones, which differ from state to state and also differ over time within the same state. Not surprisingly, then, most studies on the deterrence value of capital punishment are either inconclusive or methodologically flawed.

A case in point is the work done on this subject by the National Research Council (NRC). In 1978, they published a detailed analysis of the evidence and concluded that "available studies provide no useful evidence on the deterrent effect of capital punishment" (*Deterrence and Incapacitation*). In 2012 the NRC revisited the issue by evaluating dozens of recent studies on the issue. They found that the results of those studies varied dramatically, with some maintaining that the death penalty saves large numbers of lives, others that it increases homicides, and still others that it has no effect.

In view of these conflicting results, the NRC drew the pessimistic conclusion that research on the subject was useless for proving the issue one way or another:

The committee concludes that research to date on the effect of capital punishment on homicide is not informative about whether capital punishment decreases, increases, or has no effect on homicide rates. Therefore, the committee recommends that these studies not be used to inform deliberations requiring judgments about the effect of the death penalty on homicide. Consequently, claims that research demonstrates that capital punishment decreases or increases the homicide rate by a specified amount or has no effect on the homicide rate should not influence policy judgments about capital punishment. [NRC, Deterrence and the Death Penalty, 2012]

The NRC found two major flaws in the examined studies. First, none specified "the noncapital sanction components of the sanction regime for the punishment of homicide". That is, in evaluating the deterrence of the death penalty, the studies did not take into account the fact that the criminal was alive in prison for a lengthy period of time awaiting execution. That time in prison likely had at least some deterrence value in and of itself, but the studies failed to differentiate this from the deterrence value of the execution. This oversight, then, might have artificially inflated the deterrence value of a capital punishment program.

The second flaw in the studies was "the use of incomplete or implausible models of potential murderers' perceptions of and response to the capital punishment component of a sanction regime." That is, the studies had inadequate psychological explanations of what takes place in the minds of potential criminals when they know that the death penalty is a possible consequence of criminal conduct.

For the sake of argument, let us suppose that the death penalty has some extra deterrent value beyond imprisonment. A question still remains about how frequently it needs to be imposed to successfully deter others. Perhaps, in the best possible situation, executing five of the most dangerous convicts will result in deterring five would-be murderers in the future, and thus saving five victims' lives. As the number of executions increases, however, the number of victims' lives saved will not increase proportionally.

It may be that executing 100 criminals will still only deter five would-be murderers. According to American philosopher Hugo Adam Bedau (1926-2012), if society chooses to execute criminals because of its deterrence value, then we need to know the acceptable ratio of victims' lives saved per execution. Otherwise we may be executing hundreds of criminals with no increase in saved lives whatsoever. Bedau asks, "Would it be worth it to execute so many more murderers at the cost of such a slight decrease in social defense? How many guilty lives is one innocent life worth?" (*Matters of Life and Death*, ed. Tom Regan).

The problem, according to Bedau, though, is that we do not know what that ratio is, and it may be nearly impossible to calculate it. Thus, all that we are left with are uninformed hunches, which are not sound foundations for social policies as important as this one.

In summary, the current evidence for the deterrence value of capital punishment is weak, and defenders of the death penalty cannot draw on this in their arguments. For utilitarians, Mill's justification for capital punishment is impaired by this limitation, and, at least for now Bentham's critique, appears to be the victor in the contest between the two philosophers. We have seen that the moral arguments for capital punishment from retribution, the social contract, and rights forfeiture have their own sets of problems, and now we also find this with the utilitarian arguments. This does not mean that no successful moral argument for the death penalty exists, but the ones that we have examined so far are not compelling.

Do We Still Need the Death Penalty in Our Society?

The question of whether we still need the death penalty as a form of punishment or not in our society is one that might never be correctly answered. This is so because of the unending debates and arguments that have trailed this topic of discussion. It also appears that as long as we live, points will never run out both in support of and against retaining the capital punishment; both sides of the coin have seemingly genuine points for the stands taken on this issue, and this essay does too.

However, our aim is not to discredit anybody's opinion but rather to bring ours to the fore. It will now be left to the readers and society at large to decide on the need or otherwise of the use of capital punishment in our present age and society. This essay will, in addition to the aforementioned arguments and points on the topic of discourse, further reveal some case studies which will be critiqued below.

Credibility of the Judicial System

An initial legal issue regarding the death penalty involves the notion of proportionality, that is, whether death penalty sentences are handed down uniformly in similar situations. The issue surfaced in the Supreme Court decision *Furman v. Georgia* (1972), in which the Court ruled that the death penalty was unconstitutional because it was imposed capriciously and arbitrarily. Justice Potter Stewart famously expressed the problem here:

In the first place, it is clear that these sentences are "cruel" in the sense that they excessively go beyond, not in degree but in kind, the punishments that the state legislatures have determined to be necessary.... In the second place, it is equally clear that these sentences are "unusual" in the sense that the penalty of death is infrequently imposed for murder, and that its imposition for rape is extraordinarily rare. But I do not rest my conclusion upon these two propositions alone. These death sentences are cruel and unusual in the same way that being struck by lightning is cruel and unusual. For, of all the people convicted of rapes and murders in 1967 and 1968, many just as reprehensible as these, the petitioners are among a capriciously selected random handful upon whom the sentence of death has in fact been imposed...the Eighth and Fourteenth Amendments cannot tolerate the infliction of a sentence of death under legal systems that permit this unique penalty to be so wantonly and so freakishly imposed. [Furman v. Georgia, concurring decision]

Stewart's criticism in the above parallels Bentham's attack on the old British system of capital punishment in that it "renders convictions arbitrary" and "produces contempt for the laws". The result of this Supreme Court decision was that over 600 criminals on death row were resentenced to life imprisonment. The function of proportionality review systems is to determine whether a death sentence is consistent with the sentences imposed in factually similar cases. For example, if most people who kill someone in a bar room fight do not get executed, then it would be disproportional if I were sentenced to death for a similar crime. The challenge, though, is to devise a comprehensive list of the relevant factors in various crimes which can then be used to compare the similarity of one crime to another.

Obvious factors would include the criminal's motivation and level of violence. Less obvious factors would be whether the defendant had a troubled childhood, poor education, drug addiction, or mental impairment. Some proportionality review systems have attempted to make the comparison process as mechanical as possible. A judge or review panel would simply plug the relevant factors of a case into a statistical formula, and out would come an answer, such as whether the crime is typically punishable through death, or through long-term imprisonment. Critics of proportionality review systems charge that it is nearly impossible to make a comprehensive list of all the relevant factors and to assign to them the appropriate weight. One study concluded that "the implementation of comparative proportionality review over the last three decades has not provided, and indeed cannot provide, an adequate safeguard against the arbitrary and capricious administration of capital punishment" (Timothy V. Kaufman-Osborn, *Capital Punishment, Proportionality Review, and Claims of Fairness*, 2004).

In his book *A While Justice,* Evan Mandery tells us that after the *Furman* decision law enforcement believed crime would increase. Richard Nixon stated that he still believed in the deterrence value of the DP and hoped the *Furman* decision wouldn't preclude executing kidnappers and hijackers. Ronald Reagan said he believed the Court's ruling did not prohibit a death sentence in the case of "cold blooded, premediated, planned murder".

ARE THEY GUILTY, INNOCENT OR SOMEWHERE IN-BETWEEN

The Edward Schad Jr. Case

On Wednesday October 10, 2013, at 10 A.M., Edward Schad Jr. was executed in the Florence, Arizona State Prison, thirty-four (34) years after he was charged with murdering his victim, Lorimer Grove. The execution came two (2) hours after final appeals to the United States Supreme Court. At that time, Edward Schad, age 71, was the oldest person on Arizona's death row.

Shortly before 10 A.M., Schad was strapped to the execution table as the medical team inserted catheters into his arms to facilitate the execution process. Witnesses to the execution noted Schad joked with the medics about his good veins. With the line insertion completed more quickly than usual, the restraint team had to stand aside while Mr. Schad waited for 10 AM., the scheduled execution time. Schad is said to have chatted amicably while waiting.

When the curtain rose, the Warden read the execution warrant and Schad stated his last words to the warden as, "Well, after 34 years I'm free to fly away home. Thank you, Warden. Those are my last words". He was given a lethal dose of pentobarbital via an IV needle in both arms. Schad looked at the ceiling as the drugs coursed through his veins and he took a deep breath. Eight minutes later Edward Schad, murderer of Lorimer Grove, was pronounced dead at 10:12 AM.

Kelley Henry, attorney and federal public defender stated, "Ed Schad was a model inmate to the end" and that Shad thanked his lawyers and correctional officers who watched over him during the 35 days since his execution was scheduled, a period called "death watch," when the condemned prisoners are separated from the other inmates on death row. The Edward Schad execution was Arizona's 35th execution since 1992[1]. At that time, Schad's execution left 121

---

people on death row in Arizona, including two women. According to the Death Penalty Information Center, Viva Leroy Nash was Arizona's oldest person on death row when he died of natural causes in 2010 at the age of 94. Additionally, the oldest person in the United States to be executed since 1976 was 77-year-old John Nixon in Mississippi in 2005.

Schad says he ended up on death row only because of a misunderstanding. He was a car thief and a forger, not a murderer, he informed the Clemency Board, and his earlier second-degree murder conviction had been a case of mistaken identity as well, he said. The Clemency Board did not believe him; neither did the three juries that convicted him, nor a host of judges and justices right up to the U.S. Supreme Court over 34 years of legal appeals. Schad appealed for life in prison the week before the execution stating, "I do not have many years left but I'd like to keep what I've got and maybe get a few more." Schad's Pastor, the Reverend Ronald Koplitz, said the last statement likely was a reference to "I'll Fly Away," a Gospel song he gave Schad a couple of weeks before. The Pastor had met Schad when the Lutheran minister first arrived at the Florence, Arizona Prison in 1981 where he served as the prison Chaplin. Pastor Koplitz said he kept in touch with him after that, and gave him last rites just before the execution and also served as a witness. "He was not your typical inmate," Koplitz said. "He was a good guy. Whether he did the murder or not, I don't know," Koplitz said afterward. "He always told me he didn't, like he told everybody else."

The Juan Carlos Chavez Case

The state of Florida conducted the execution of confessed murderer Juan Carlos Chavez on February 12, 2014. The accused confessed, and stood trial for, the 1995 rape, murder, and dismemberment of nine (9) year-old Jimmy Ryce.

In the Juan Carlos Chavez Case, 9-year-old Jimmy Ryce was kidnapped from his school bus and led by gunpoint to Chavez's trailer. He then raped the young boy and shot him when the boy tried to escape. Chavez panicked, then proceeded to cut the boy's body into several small pieces and hid the pieces in cement planters. All this while his parents and search parties were combing the area in desperation to find the youth.

Jimmy's brother, Ted Ryce, attended the execution of his brother's killer, according to the Florida's Sun-Sentinel. He was quoted as saying, "Many people have asked why I decided to come today. I did not come today to celebrate Juan Carlos's execution…. Many people did not believe that Juan Carlos Chavez should be put to death for his horrible crime of raping and murdering my brother Jimmy Ryce. I believe this comes from a place of weakness, not strength. It comes from not being able to face the atrociousness of some men's actions and punish them on a level commensurate with their crime." He added, "But we must be strong. We must do what it takes to send a clear message to other child predators that if they go after children, if they kill children, that they will die at the executioner's hands. Today will bring no closure for my family. As my father has stated, 'Closure does not exist,' but the justice served this day after a painful 19 years will end the chapter on this part of our life and now we look forward to moving on."

The Suzanne Basso Case

Suzanne Basso, convicted of torturing and killing a mentally impaired man she lured to Texas with the promise of marriage, was put to death on February 5, 2014 in a rare execution of a female prisoner fifteen years after the murder.

The lethal injection of Suzanne Basso, 59, made the New York native only the 14th woman executed in the U.S. since the Supreme Court allowed capital punishment to resume in 1976. Almost 1,400 men have been put to death during that time.

Before being put to death, Basso told a warden who stood near her, "No sir," when asked to make a final statement. She appeared to be holding back tears, then smiled at two friends watching through a window. She mouthed a brief word to them and nodded.

As the lethal dose of pentobarbital took effect, Basso, dressed in a white prison uniform, began to snore. Her deep snoring became less audible and eventually stopped.

She was pronounced dead at 6:26 p.m. CST, 11 minutes after the drug was administered.

Basso was sentenced to die for the 1998 slaying of 59-year-old Louis "Buddy" Musso, whose battered and lacerated body, washed with bleach and scoured with a wire brush, was found in a ditch outside Houston. Prosecutors said Basso had made herself the beneficiary of Musso's insurance policies and took over his Social Security benefits after luring him from New Jersey.

The execution took place on February 5, 2014, some fifteen years after the Musso murder. In a last-minute effort, the Supreme Court rejected a last-day appeal from Basso's attorney who argued she was not mentally competent. Lower federal courts and state courts also refused to halt the punishment, upholding the findings of a state judge last month that Basso had a history of fabricating stories about herself, seeking attention and manipulating psychological tests.

Leading up to her trial, Basso's court appearances were marked by claims of blindness and paralysis, and speech mimicking a little girl.

"It was challenging, but I saw her for who she was," said Colleen Barnett, the former Harris County assistant district attorney who prosecuted Basso. "I was determined I was not going to let her get away with it."

Basso's attorney, Winston Cochran Jr., argued she suffered from delusions and that the state law governing competency was unconstitutionally flawed. Her lawyer said a degenerative disease left her paralyzed, but Basso, who used a wheelchair, blamed her paralysis on a jail beating years ago. At a competency hearing two months ago, she testified from a hospital bed wheeled into a Houston courtroom and talked about a snake smuggled into a prison hospital in an attempt to kill her.

But she acknowledged lying about her background, including that she was a triplet, worked in the New York governor's office and had a relationship with Nelson Rockefeller. She originally was from the Albany and Schenectady areas of New York.

Prosecutors said Musso was living in New Jersey when he met either Basso or her son at a church carnival, then moved to Jacinto City, east of Houston, with an offer of marriage. Evidence showed Basso was already married but took over Musso's benefits and insurance.

An autopsy showed Musso had several broken bones, including a skull fracture and 14 broken ribs. His back was covered with cigarette burns, and bruises were found all over his body.

Basso became a suspect after reporting Musso missing following the discovery of his body. Five others also were convicted, including Basso's son, but prosecutors only sought the death penalty for Basso.

"Suzanne ran the show for sure. ... She was the one in charge. She directed them. She wanted the money," Barnett said. "She's a heinous killer."

Among witnesses testifying at Basso's punishment trial was her daughter, who told of emotional, physical and sexual abuse at the hands of her mother.

Executing the Innocent

Throughout history there have been concerns about innocent people being wrongfully executed. As Justice Stewart stated, "The penalty of death differs from all other forms of criminal punishment, not in degree, but in kind. It is unique in its total irrevocability" (*Furman v. Georgia*). Evidence has shown that many inmates on death row were in fact innocent of the crimes they were convicted of, or at least accused of based on faulty evidence.

1.   In 1944, George Stinney was electrocuted after a 3-hour trial for the murders of two white girls. There was no physical evidence, no witnesses and no appeal. Legal justice was a long time coming in the case of Stinney, a fourteen-year-old black boy in rural South Carolina who became the youngest person executed in modern times.

In 2014, Judge Carmen Mullins vacated the boy's conviction and cleared his name for the beating death of Mary Emma Thames, aged 7, and Betty June Binnicker, aged 11, in segregated Alcolu, South Carolina. The girls had been riding their bicycles when they disappeared in 1944 and their bodies were later found in a watery ditch on the black side of town, apparently attacked with a railroad spike.

Judge Mullins found "fundamental, constitutional violations of due process." She noted the lack of a credible defense during trial and said the boy's confession, which had two versions, appeared to have been coursed and there were no witnesses and physical evidence in the case.

The victims' families however opposed vacating the conviction, saying very little remained in the way of physical records for the trial, and that it would be impossible to determine exactly what happened decades ago in the Deep South Court room. The trial was said to have lasted for only three hours and it took only 10 minutes for an all-white, all-male jury to convict Stinney. He was sent to the electric chair not quite three months later.

2.   An Arkansas trial judge dismissed all charges against former death-row prisoner, Rickey Dale Newman, setting him free on October 11 after having spent nearly 17 years in custody following the February 2001 murder of a transient woman in a "hobo park" on the outskirts of Van Buren, Arkansas. Newman became the 160th person since 1973 to be exonerated after being wrongly convicted and sentenced to death.

Newman, a former Marine with major depression, chronic post-traumatic stress disorder from childhood abuse, and an IQ in the intellectually disabled range, was severely mentally ill and homeless at the time he was charged with murdering Marie Cholette. He was convicted and sentenced to death in June 2002 after a one-day trial in which the court permitted him to represent himself. No physical evidence linked Newman to the murder, but at trial a prosecution expert falsely testified that hair found on Newman's clothing came from the victim. Newman also told the jury he had committed the murder and asked them to impose the death penalty. He subsequently sought to waive his appeals and be executed.

The Arkansas Supreme Court initially held that Newman had been mentally competent and granted his request to drop his appeals. However, four days before his scheduled execution on July 26, 2005, Newman permitted federal public defenders, including his current counsel, Julie Brain, to seek a stay of execution. DNA evidence on the blanket on which the victim was found excluded Newman, and the federal defenders obtained DNA testing of the hair evidence that disproved the prosecution's trial testimony. They also discovered that prosecutors had withheld from the defense evidence from the murder scene that contradicted what Newman had described in his confession.

A federal court hearing disclosed that the state mental health doctor had made significant errors in administering and scoring tests he had relied upon for his testimony that Newman had been competent to stand trial. The Arkansas Supreme Court subsequently ordered new hearings on Newman's competency and on the evidence the prosecution had withheld from the defense. After those hearings, they wrote that "the record overwhelmingly illustrates that Newman's cognitive deficits and mental illnesses interfered with his ability to effectively and rationally assist counsel" and overturned Newman's conviction.

In September, it issued another ruling barring the use of Newman's incompetent confessions in any retrial. On October 2, Brain submitted a letter to the court saying that "Mr. Newman has now been incarcerated for over 16 years for a murder that he did not commit" and that the Arkansas Supreme Court had found that the invalid statements he had given while mentally incompetent were "the only meaningful evidence against him." In response, special prosecutor Ron Fields submitted a letter to the court asking that charges be dismissed. Fields wrote that, without the confessions, prosecutors lacked sufficient evidence to obtain a conviction and "it would be a waste of tax payers' money to retry [Newman]."

Let us a take a close look at both case histories above: The first had an innocent young lad executed and exonerated in name seventy years later while the second almost had a man killed based on a wrongful accusation only to be later found innocent. Another interesting thing to note about both scenarios is that the trial was void of convincing evidence and while one had no physical evidence or witness, the other had a false witness in session. How then are we sure that people that have been executed in the past were fairly tried?

The criminal justice system has been said to be so flawed that innocent people are regularly given the death penalty, while many steps can be taken to improve the system, given human frailty, one can ever guarantee that only the guilty will be executed, and this has sparked a national debate on the issue. Judges are believed to be mostly anxious to point out, and juries to allow for, the barest possibility of the prisoner's innocence. Is it not better that ten-guilty people should escape than one innocent person should suffer?

Although the defenders of the death penalty have argued that there is no absolute proof that any innocent person has been executed in recent decades, death penalty opponents recognize the difficulty in definitively naming innocent people who have been executed, and much of the reason for this, they argue, is that in most capital punishment cases there is no DNA evidence available from the crime scene.

Nevertheless, the fact remains that many people on death row have been proven innocent through DNA testing. An organization called the Innocence Project is devoted to setting free wrongfully convicted people with the help of such tests, most of whom, they explain, "are poor, forgotten, and have used up all legal avenues for relief." It is unreasonable to think that we have so far been lucky enough to rescue every innocent person from death row. Indeed, as the survey cited at the outset indicates, most people in the U.S. believe that innocent people have been executed.

Racial Bias

1.   Thomas Griffin and Meeks Griffin, two black men, were convicted of the murder of a white man because Monk Stevenson, another black man

suspected of committing the murder, stated that the brothers were responsible for the murder. He later admitted that the reason he blamed them is because they were wealthy and he assumed that they had the money to fight the charges. They were completely innocent but put to death nonetheless.

2.   Rodney Reed, a black man, was convicted in Texas by an all-white jury in the rape and murder of Stacey Stites, a 19-year-old white woman. Reed has been on Texas death role since 1998. The prosecution case against Reed was simple: His DNA was found inside Stites's murdered body; therefore, he must have killed her even though his semen was the only physical evidence that linked him to the crime. His finger prints were not on Stites' truck, nor were they on the belt used by the perpetrator to strangle her. There were no hairs, no other biological evidence and no witnesses who had seen them together. It was just the DNA, which Reed explained was not from the day

for her death but from a sexual encounter with Stites the day before her murder.

Reed consistently claimed that he had been sexually involved with Stites for months before her death and that he had nothing whatsoever to do with her murder. However, at trial, the lawyers did very little to establish his relationship with Stites, even though there were multiple witnesses who could attested to that relationship. There was also another clear suspect: A white police officer and Stites's fiancé, Jimmy Fennel. As one witness, Mary Blackwell told the court, Fennel once said during a police academic class that he would strangle his girlfriend with a belt if she cheated on him, and she was indeed strangled to death by belt.

Fennel was later convicted in an unrelated kidnapping and sexual assault of a 20-year-old woman, but the police focused on Reed as a suspect, as they never searched the apartment shared by Fennel and Stites. They also returned the truck to Fennel six days after the murder and before full forensic testing was complete. Fennel promptly sold the truck and any potential evidence that went with it.

3.   George Stinney, as stated above under *Executing the Innocent*, was convicted by an all-white, all-male jury in a trial that lasted for only three hours and had no physical evidence and no witnesses.

The lack of physical evidence as shown in the three cases above is deeply troubling, but so is the racial bias that pervaded every aspect of the cases. In the case of the Griffin brothers, the jury decided to sentence both to death based on the account of a *fellow black man* without waiting to consider other options of investigation and prosecution. In the second example, the bias started with a taboo of an inter-racial relationship in a small town in Texas and was compounded by an all-white jury as seen in Stinney's case; it was consistent with the disturbing pattern of racial disparity found in so many capital cases involving a black defendant and a white victim.

Jessica S. Henry, in her October, 2015 blog, states that "Reed's case is a classic textbook example of how innocent black people wind up on death row: bad lawyering, the failure of the police to investigate other leads, possible prosecutorial misconduct, junk forensic science and perhaps most significantly, the taint of racial bias".

4.   Kirk Bloodsworth, a former Marine and waterman on the Eastern Shore of Maryland, was the first person to be sentenced to death and then subsequently exonerated from death row by a post-conviction DNA. In June1993 he was released from death row and pardoned in December 1993 after having been accused of the July 25th 1984 rape and murder of nine-year old Dawn Hamilton.

Although there was no physical evidence connecting him to the crime Bloodsworth was convicted mainly on the testimony of five witnesses who said they had seen Kirk with the victim as well as an anonymous call telling police that he was seen with the victim that day and an identification made by a witness from a police sketch shown on television.

In the early 1990s, Bloodsworth learned about DNA testing and the opportunities it could provide to prove one's innocence. The prosecution finally agreed to DNA testing for Bloodworth's case in 1992. The victim's shorts and underwear, a stick found at the scene, and an autopsy slide were compared against DNA from the victim and Bloodsworth. The DNA lab determined that testing on the panties excluded Bloodsworth as well as replicate testing performed by the FBI that yielded the same results.

Inhumane Methods of Execution

1.   Calling   eyewitness   accounts "horrifying," attorneys for Arkansas prisoner Kenneth Williams are seeking the   preservation   of   evidence   and   "a full investigation"   into   what   they   described   as Williams's "problematic execution."

Williams's attorney, Shawn Nolan, said the lawyers had "tried over and over again to get the state to comport with their own protocol to avoid torturing our client to death, and yet reports from the execution witnesses indicate that Mr. Williams suffered during this execution." Media witnesses reported that they observed Williams "coughing, convulsing, lurching, jerking, with sound that was audible even with the microphone turned off" during his execution.

According to Associated Press reporter Kelly Kissel, "Williams's body jerked 15 times in quick succession — lurching violently against the leather restraint across his chest." Kissel, who has witnessed ten executions, said, "This is the most I've seen an inmate move three or four minutes in." Nolan called the situation "very disturbing, but not at all surprising, given the history of the risky sedative midazolam, which has been used in many botched executions."

A spokesperson for Arkansas Governor Asa Hutchinson dismissed the witness accounts, calling the execution "flawless" and Williams's movement an "involuntary muscular reaction." Nolan characterized the spokesperson's statement as "simply trying to whitewash the reality of what happened." Williams was the fourth person executed in Arkansas in eight days.

The state had originally planned to execute eight inmates in eleven days, but courts stayed four of the executions for reasons specific to those prisoners. Experts, including former correctional officials, had warned that the rushed execution schedule increased the risk of problematic executions, and attorneys for the prisoners challenged the use of midazolam as the first drug in the three-drug execution protocol, arguing it would not adequately anesthetize the prisoner. Three days before Kenneth Williams's execution, problems were reported in the Arkansas execution of Jack Jones, but a federal judge allowed the state to proceed with the execution of Marcel Williams on the same night.

2.   According to an independent expert who reviewed the official autopsy report of Ricky Gray's death, something went wrong during his execution when he was put to death in Virginia on January 18, 2017.

Dr. Mark Edgar, associate director of bone and soft tissue pathology at the Emory University School of Medicine, reviewed the official autopsy report, which Gray's family obtained from the Virginia medical examiner's office. Dr. Edgar says Gray suffered an acute pulmonary edema during the execution, with liquid in his upper airways and blood entering his lungs while he was still breathing. "The anatomic changes described in Ricky Gray's lungs are more often seen in the aftermath of a sarin gas attack than in a routine hospital autopsy" Edgar said. "This is of concern especially given the fact that midazolam is not an aesthetic, but a sedative often used for medical procedures requiring conscious sedation and the issue that the compounded drugs used in this case may have lacked potency or been impure."

Virginia's lethal injection protocol consists of three drugs: midazolam, a sedative intended to render the prisoner unconscious, followed by a paralytic intended to stop the prisoner's breathing, followed by potassium chloride, which stops the prisoner's heart. The use of midazolam in executions is controversial because it is not an anesthetic; it is used in medical settings only for lower levels of sedation rather than to produce full unconsciousness, and its use has been linked to numerous problematic executions.

In Virginia, both midazolam and potassium chloride are produced by compounding pharmacies whose identities are secret under state law. "This way of dying is intolerable. You can't control your breathing—it is terrible," Edgar said. "When it is this severe, you can experience panic and terror and, if the individual was in any way aware of what was happening to them, it would be unbearable."

After Edgar's report was released on July 6, lawyers for William Morva—whose execution was scheduled in Virginia that night—asked Governor Terry McAuliffe for a temporary reprieve. "We believed a reprieve was appropriate to allow time for further investigation to ensure that the Commonwealth carries out future executions—including Mr. Morva's—in a manner that avoids unnecessary pain and suffering," explained Rob Lee, one of Morva's attorneys. McAuliffe denied the reprieve, and witnesses reported that Morva made a loud noise after the midazolam was administered and had several sharp contractions of his abdomen. The same three-drug protocol used in Virginia has been proposed for use in Ohio, but is being challenged in court by death-row prisoners.

3.   Brian Lyman reported the recent execution of Torrey McNabb in Alabama on October 19, 2017, amid questions of state interference in the judicial

process, resulting in another apparent failure by the drug midazolam to render a prisoner insensate during the execution.

Alabama prison officials defended the execution—which took 35 minutes—as conforming with state protocol, most of which has been withheld from the public. *Montgomery Advertiser* execution witness Brian Lyman reported that at 9:17 p.m., twenty minutes into the execution and after two consciousness checks, "McNabb raised his right arm and rolled his head in a grimace" and then fell "back on the gurney."

Associated Press also reported that his "family members and attorneys who witnessed the execution expressed repeated concerns to each other that he was still conscious during the lethal injection." Alabama Department of Corrections Commissioner Jeff Dunn dismissed McNabb's responses as involuntary movement, which he said was not unusual: "I'm confident he was more than unconscious at that point," he said.

 McNabb had been challenging the state's execution protocol in court for more than a year at the time Alabama issued a warrant for his execution. He had won an appeal permitting his case against the state's use of midazolam to move forward to trial, and the Alabama federal courts had issued an injunction stopping the execution so that judicial review of the state's execution process could take place.

However, on October 19, the U.S. Supreme Court, over the dissents of Justices Breyer and Sotomayor, lifted the injunction, vacating the stay and permitting the execution to proceed. Two-and-a-half hours after the execution was scheduled to begin, the Supreme Court denied another last-minute stay application, without dissent, and the execution proceeded. The execution capped a dramatic 48 hours during which Texas courts halted two other executions that had been scheduled for October.

On October 18, the Texas Court of Criminal Appeals had stayed Clinton Young's October 26 execution to permit an evidentiary hearing on his challenge that newly discovered gunshot residue evidence showed that the state's lead witness was the actual killer in his case. Additionally, a Texas trial court had stayed the execution of Anthony Shore to investigate allegations that he may have colluded with another death-row prisoner to falsely confess to the murder for which that prisoner had been condemned. McNabb's execution was Alabama's third and the 21st in the United States in 2017.

The question to be asked in relation to the three scenarios explained above is, 'Does anyone deserve to die such a painful death?' People may argue that in most cases, the criminals to be executed are most likely to have been convicted of gruesome murder cases and thus deserve to die in less humane circumstances, but does that not make us murderers too?

It is surprising that lethal injection is considered as the most humane form of execution and thus replaced other methods such as electrocution, hanging, lethal gas and the cruel early methods of incapacitation, death by a thousand cuts, burning, etc. The question then is that if this form of execution which is regarded as *better* includes testimonies of agony and pain, how would it have been with the earlier forms that are considered more gruesome?

Even the drugs used in the execution processes were originally not manufactured for such a purpose; they were to be used in the cure and management of health conditions and not to take lives. States in the U.S have had to change from the single drug dose, sodium thiopental, pentobarbital and then propofol- the powerful operating room anesthetic infamous for its role in Michael Jackson's overdose death - to the three-drug method presently used over manufacturers' prohibition that the drugs should not be used in executions.

It has also been recently revealed that these states are beginning to run out of drugs used in executions and are currently using compounding pharmacies to turn out custom-made drugs. Is the cost and stress involved in getting these drugs worth it? The suggestion in this case is that other forms of punishment like life imprisonment without parole be given to criminals instead.

People's Opinion

It is of interest that in a 2010 poll by Lake Research Partners, a clear majority of voters (63%) would choose a punishment other than the death penalty for murder. The results showed: Life without parole plus restitution (39%), death penalty (33%), life without parole (13%), and life with parole (9%). Some view the death penalty as a deterrence, as disclosed in a 2009 poll commissioned by the Death Penalty Information Centre (DPIC). However, it should be noted that police chiefs ranked the death penalty last among ways to reduce crime and viewed the death penalty as the least effective use of taxpayers' money.

For example, the anti-capital punishment campaigning group Reprieve quotes figures which suggest that countries with the death penalty tend to have higher homicide rates. They claimed last year: "The five countries in the world with the highest homicide rates that do not impose the death penalty have nearly half the number of murders per 100,000 people than the five countries with the highest homicides rates which do impose the death penalty" (United Nations Development Program).

The validity of using static murder rates as a means of determining the penalty's deterrent effect is of course open to question. While the figures could lead one to conclude that capital punishment is ineffective given the high murder rates in countries where it is legal, it could also be the case that the countries which do practice it would have much higher homicide rates if the death penalty were not in place.

Homicide rates have, however, proven to be a common measure of deterrence in the United States, and have also been the basis of detailed research on the matter. In light of this, Full Fact decided to test the claim that countries with the death penalty tend to have higher homicide rates on average, using the latest United Nations data: The five countries with the highest homicide rates who also have legal capital punishment are Jamaica, El Salvador*, Guatemala, Trinidad & Tobago and Lesotho, with an average between them of 46.6 homicides per 100,000 people. Meanwhile the five such countries who have abolished the death penalty for all crimes are Honduras, Venezuela, Colombia, South Africa and Ecuador, with an average homicide rate of 41.3 per 100,000 people. This, however, is far more than half the number of murders amongst the five countries with the penalty still in force. Taking average homicide rates of all countries with and without the death penalty, the difference is marginally greater, with 36.7 homicides per 100,000 amongst those with the death penalty compared to 27.4 amongst those which abolished it.

Finally, Full Fact calculated if there was any correlation between countries imposing a death penalty and having higher homicide rates, as the averages would suggest. Ranking all 147 countries for which data was available in terms of homicide rate and comparing this to whether the penalty existed or not yielded a weak positive correlation of 0.2.

This means that there is some correlation between imposing the death penalty and having higher homicide rates, but this correlation is in fact weak to bordering on insignificant. So, it seems that those using global homicide rates to support either side of the death penalty debate need to justify why their findings are statistically significant. Calculations suggest there isn't enough proof that capital punishment is or isn't an effective deterrent to murder.

Financial Costs Death Penalty vs Life in Prison

Financial costs from a humanitarian point should be our least concern. However, some individuals are concerned about the financial costs of the death penalty vs life in prison. McFarland, in his book *The Death Penalty vs. Life Incarceration: A Financial Analysis* (2016), discloses, "Overall, the death penalty is more expensive in almost every aspect than simply incarcerating a prisoner for the entirety of his or her life."

The Death Penalty Information Center (DPIC) reports a new study of California's death penalty found that taxpayers have spent more than $4 billion on capital punishment since it was reinstated in 1978, or $308 million for each of the 13 executions carried out since then. The study, conducted by U.S. Court of Appeals Judge Arthur L. Alarcon and Loyola Law School Professor Paula M. Mitchell estimated that capital trials, enhanced security on death row and legal representation for capital defendants add $184 million to California's budget annually. California has the largest death row in the country and has not had an execution since 2006 due to legal challenges to its lethal injection protocol. The report's authors concluded that unless profound (and costlier) reforms are made, the capital punishment system will continue to exist mostly in theory while exacting an untenable cost. Judge Alarcon and Professor Mitchell forecast the cost of maintaining the death penalty will increase to $9 billion by 2030, when the state's death row will likely grow to well over 1,000 inmates.

Michael Millman, Executive Director of the California Appellate Project, said more than 300 inmates on death row are waiting to be appointed attorneys for their state appeals and federal habeas corpus petitions. Millman said there are fewer than 100 attorneys in the state who are qualified to handle capital cases because the work is dispiriting and demanding, and the compensation inadequate.

Justin Marceau and Hollis Whitson, in their report *The Cost of Colorado's Death Penalty*, disclosed the cost of Colorado's death penalty in court days. They compare the number of days in court and the actual length of time from charges until sentencing in death prosecutions and first-degree murder cases with similarly egregious facts. They found that death prosecutions require substantially more days in court and take substantially longer to resolve than non-death-prosecuted first-degree murder cases that result in a sentence of life imprisonment without parole. Moreover, the costs of these prosecutions are not offset by any tangible benefit. The study showed that not only are death penalty prosecutions costly compared to non-death cases, but the threat of the death penalty at the charging stage does not save costs by resulting in speedier pleas when the defendant wants to avoid the death penalty. In addition, the substantial cost of the death penalty cannot be justified by the possibility of future deterrence insofar as social scientists increasingly agree that the deterrence benefits of the death penalty are entirely speculative. In short, by compiling and analyzing original data, they show that Colorado's death penalty imposes a major cost without yielding any measurable benefits. Marceau, Justin F., and Hollis A. Whitson. "The Cost of Colorado's Death Penalty." University of Denver Criminal Law Review 3 (2013): 145-63.

Aggravating Factors

Aggravating factors (AF) for the death penalty differ from state to state, and especially so in the case of the murder of law enforcement officers and first responders. The state of Alabama for example considers the murder of any of the following an AF: a police officer, sheriff, deputy, state trooper, federal law enforcement officer, or any other state or federal peace officer of any kind, or prison or jail guard while such officer or guard is on duty, regardless of whether the defendant knew or should have known the victim was an officer or guard on duty, or because of some official or job-related act or performance of such officer or guard. The state of California considers it an AF when the victim was a peace officer...who, while engaged in the course of the performance of his or her duties, was intentionally killed, and the defendant knew, or reasonably should have known, that the victim was a peace officer engaged in the performance of his or her duties; or the victim was a peace officer...or a former peace officer under any of those sections, and was intentionally killed in retaliation for the performance of his or her official duties. The state of Delaware had an AF statute if the murder was committed against any law-enforcement officer, corrections employee, firefighter, paramedic, emergency medical technician, fire marshal or fire police officer while said victim was engaged in the performance of official duties. However, on August 2, 2016, the Delaware Supreme Court held that the state's capital sentencing procedures were unconstitutional and struck down Delaware's death penalty statute. On August 15, the Delaware Attorney

General's office announced that it would not appeal the Supreme Court's ruling. So, we see again, as in other policies, even in the case of 'special circumstances' a lack of an interstate or federal policy protection for our law enforcement first line of defense is divided. Arguments can be made that we must protect those who protect us. Or, where does it end?

In reference to the administration of the death penalty sanctioned by a government there is the possible problem of a stigma imprint on the world court scene. Some visualize the death penalty as a brutal process and thus express concerns that it is not moral for a country to put to death a human being as a punishment for killing another. Some believe the death penalty only serves to bring out the worst in us, and in some cases only to satisfy a political agenda. Simply put, what does it say about the socialization of a country or government when you put individuals to death for killing other individuals? Is there not a more satisfying punishment than a government being committed to the act of execution?

Citizens and law makers who question the death penalty as a form of punishment must take a position on whether to abolish, retain, or change it while considering that the present continued use of capital punishment is logically difficult as both sides have seemingly genuine points of disagreement.

Some have suggested a compromise might be made by making the judicial system more just and less prone to the error of executing innocent people, which is perhaps due to a lack of proper investigation and antiquated laws. In any circumstance, each case should be treated based on its own merits and carefully examined before judgements are passed.

Questions should be addressed regarding more humane methods of execution so as to forestall more cases of painful and torturous deaths if the death penalty is an elected choice. Until then, life without parole is possible as well as modifications to either sentence.

65289350R00156

Made in the USA
Middletown, DE
26 February 2018